CULTURE OF THE
KINGDOM

A JOURNEY OF RESTORATION

By Peter Tsukahira

CULTURE OF THE KINGDOM

A Journey of Restoration

Peter Tsukahira

CULTURE OF THE KINGDOM
A Journey of Restoration

Copyright © 2012 by Peter Tsukahira

All scripture quotations, unless otherwise indicated, are taken from the New American Standard Bible®, ©Copyright 1960, 1962, 1963, 1968, 1971, 1972, 1973, 1975, 1977, 1995 by The Lockman Foundation (www.Lockman.org). Used by permission.

NOTE:
In this book, the word "Spirit" is capitalized whenever it directly refers to the Holy Spirit. "Law" is capitalized when it specifically means the Torah, the Law of Israel.

ISBN 978-965-91110-1-5

Carmel Communications

For Rita.
Without you this story
would never have been told.

INTRODUCTION

L ater in life, our eyesight often changes. Many experience an increasing farsightedness where things in the distance are easier to see while things close up become less distinct. In a similar way, the more time passes from events that took place earlier in my life, the better I understand their significance. This story is about looking back at some of the important people and places that shaped my journey of faith and what I learned about the culture of God's kingdom along the way.

In 1959, the government of the then Soviet Union presented to the United Nations headquarters in New York City a sculpture created by Russian artist Yevgeny Vuchetich called, "Let Us Beat Swords into Plowshares." The heroic bronze figure is of a man with a hammer in one hand powerfully beating a sword blade into a plowshare. The sculpture, which came to be one of the symbols of hope for peace during the Cold War, is based on a verse from the second chapter of Isaiah:

> *And He will judge between the nations, and will render*
> *decisions for many peoples; and they will hammer their*

swords into plowshares and their spears into pruning
hooks. Nation will not lift up sword against nation, and
never again will they learn war. (Isaiah 2:4)

Sadly, the phrase, "beat swords into plowshares" was taken out of context, and the full meaning of the scripture was lost to the public. Isaiah the prophet wrote that when God is established as ruler of the nations and His Law goes forth from Zion that He will judge between the peoples and the world will know the meaning of true peace. The preceding verses in Isaiah are as follows:

Now it will come about that in the last days the mountain
of the house of the LORD will be established as the chief
of the mountains, and will be raised above the hills; and
all the nations will stream to it. And many peoples will
come and say, "Come, let us go up to the mountain of the
LORD, To the house of the God of Jacob; That He may
teach us concerning His ways And that we may walk in
His paths." For the law will go forth from Zion and the
word of the LORD from Jerusalem. (Isaiah 2:2-3)

Isaiah's inspired prophecy states that towards the end of human history the nations will stream to the house of the God of Jacob. They will be drawn there because of a unique treasure unavailable elsewhere – the teaching of God's ways. Specifically, it is God's word in the form of His Law that they will come seeking like a pearl of great price, higher in value than anything else the nations might possess. God's Law, which is inseparable from His reign as King, will restore the nations to God's original plan as prosperous and peaceful domains. Implements of war will be transformed into bountiful means of production. The prophet Isaiah captured God's vision for the future. The pages that follow are about the present day restoration of biblical truth and my own discoveries along the frontier where God's kingdom meets the cultures of the nations.

TABLE OF CONTENTS

CHAPTER 1

CHAPTER 1

When I was a teenager, the three major cultural influences in my life were the plays of Jean Paul Sartre, the movie *Blow-Up* directed by Michaelangelo Antonioni, and the music of Bob Dylan.

Dylan sang:
God said to Abraham, "Kill me a son."
Abe said, "Man, you must be puttin' me on."
God said, "No."
Abe say, "What?"
God said, "You can do what you want, Abe, but the next time you see me comin' you better run."

It was the mid-1960s, and I was under the earphones in my parents' home listening to a new record a friend had lent me. Bob Dylan's "Highway 61 Revisited" was ringing in my ears and rearranging my mind. I had never read the words in the book of Genesis about the sacrificial offering of Isaac and God's command to Abraham, but I understood what Dylan was saying. The sheer defiance of it was speaking directly to my teen-aged soul.

A couple years before that at the age of thirteen I had come to a realization. I had been confirmed in the Episcopalian church, which meant that after a series of religion classes the bishop came and prayed over me. What I realized was more than just that I didn't believe in God. I also understood that no one I knew in my church believed in Him. We uttered the prayers and took the sacraments, but from my point of view, no one actually lived as though they believed God was really there at all.

When I was sixteen, two things happened to me that looking back were like spiritual milestones on the unfolding journey of my young adulthood. The first was a *Time* magazine cover in April 1966 that asked in bold red letters on a black background, "Is God Dead?" I don't remember what was in the article or if I even read it. I do remember thinking, "Why is this an issue? It doesn't matter if God is dead. Anyway, He's irrelevant!" The second event was a movie. Michelangelo Antonioni's movie *Blow-Up* premiered that year, and I saw it in the summertime.

It was a movie about a photographer in London who accidentally photographs what he later thinks is the evidence of a murder. He blows up the pictures and goes back to the scene and sees the body of a dead man. Returning to his studio, he finds his pictures missing. Eventually, he comes to question whether any of it took place at all. It wasn't so much the plot that was intriguing; it was another message transmitting from the background that captivated me. It was about another reality that was cool, exciting and characterized by sex, drugs and rock 'n' roll. That movie was my entry point into the counterculture of the 1960s.

An English blues group called The Yardbirds was in *Blow-Up*. They were in one scene where lead guitarist Jeff Beck smashes his electric guitar and throws it into the crowd while guitarist number two, Jimmy Page, (who later went on to fame with the band Led Zeppelin) plays on unfazed. The people in the club begin fighting in a frenzy over the neck of the ruined guitar. The photographer emerges with the prize and runs from the club. Arriving on the sidewalk outside, after a few paces, he tosses the splintered trophy away like a piece of trash. This scene epitomized the nihilistic attitude projected on the screen of my young heart by the film.

Arriving at Tufts University in the fall of 1968, entering freshmen were greeted by upperclassmen handing out flyers that read, "Welcome to Maggie's Farm." It was a reference to Bob Dylan's song about underground life in New York City. The point being that university was not to be an ivory tower of advanced learning but rather a hotbed of protest against establishment hypocrisy. There was the traditional university of courses, classes, and credits and the alternative one. In the alternative university there were roughly two tracks. One was radical politics, and the other psychedelic drugs and rock music. I opted for the latter and zealously began to apply myself to learning its ways and means.

Sartre's influence was harder to identify. The existentialists taught us that life was meaningless and absurd; however, in the face of it, a man had to make courageous choices that made him real. At the university I made a friend named John. He was brilliant and a dreamer. He wanted to write poetry, but no one took him seriously until his originality was noticed by a few of the faculty. Soon, he was a leader of our small circle of friends. John was a young man of conscience and tried to live what he believed. That's what made him a leader and someone we admired. When I hurt myself by jumping through a window on an LSD trip and ended up in the university clinic, John sat up with me all night. He had a girlfriend named Kathy, but when they broke up, he lost one of the beacons that was guiding his own young life.

Sometime later, John said to me that he didn't think it was possible to live a "good" life. I asked him what he meant by "good," and he answered that "good" was what you knew was right. He said he could become a "negative guru," someone who fakes everything and purposefully misleads others, but the idea of that filled him with self contempt. I said that no one lives a good life and that everyone had to compromise in order to survive. He said that in his opinion survival was not that important.

16

In all our youthful wisdom we were trying to answer the question: Why live? Was it to find perfect love? To create a world without injustice? To mold a better society? Our once bold questions had begun to seem like a bad joke. We had set off with the infinite knowledge and optimism of youth, but we couldn't imagine that we were mostly the products of our parents' culture. Even though the Vietnam War was winding down, and the body count was dwindling, another war was raging in our minds. It was a war fought to justify our own "free" existence. My friend John dared to ask the question, "What if everyone else in the world was wrong, but we were no better or even worse?" In the face of a world without truth, a universe terrifyingly silent to his plea for an answer, he had made a decision. If there was no good reason to live, then he simply wouldn't. John tried to crash his car into a bridge spanning a major highway around Boston.

John and I had argued about his decision in the cold Cambridge apartment we shared. Others tried to help. Psychiatrists and professional counselors had been involved at one time or another. His problem was that the futility he felt was deeply anguishing, but it was more than a feeling that could be analyzed. For him it was a fact of life, and he discovered that he was less afraid of dying than most of the people who talked to him. He approached his predicament with the sorrowful courage of an existentialist and wrote about it in poetic words tinged with youthful hope. Years later, a philosopher friend from Jerusalem would comment that John was simply refusing to become a cynic.

My friend Rita was working for a Gestalt therapist in Cambridge and together we knew of various places that offered psychological/spiritual healing. John withdrew all the money in his bank account, and we sat one afternoon trying to decide where we could go to find help—a reason for him to live. We smoked a lot of cigarettes and marijuana that day. Somehow we came to the conclusion that the answer we sought was a person, not a place, and that if that person were to come to the door, we would all recognize him and the search would be over. We had no idea who that person could be.

John went to his mother's home in Denver and fearing he would take his life, Rita and I went along. One day, he asked me to accompany him in his mother's Volvo on a drive. We drove east out of town for a while and, in those days after passing by Aurora, there was nothing but empty fields. Today, it is probably all built up with suburbs, and off to the south there are communities like Littleton, where Columbine High School is located. Unknowingly, we were being drawn, as if by an ocean current, into what has become a riptide of violence in America. As we drove, John showed me a pistol he had purchased at a local pawn shop. He said this would be the day he was going to die. My pulse began beating faster; my mind started racing. Now at last, we had come to the real thing. I was the only one who knew what he was planning. I was his friend.

18

What should I do? What could I do?

He drove off the road into a field, and we got out of the car. I asked to see the cheap, shiny silver "Saturday night special" revolver and when it was in my hand, I knew I couldn't just stand by passively. I had to do something. I was there—not someone else and not somewhere else. I was responsible. I stammered and then shouted at him, "Do you want me to shoot you?" He said calmly, "No, that would be murder." Just then, the question passed through my mind, "What if I killed myself?" Would that act somehow obligate him to live, for my sake? Immediately, I knew it wouldn't work. I'd have no guarantee that he wouldn't just use a second bullet to make it a double suicide.   In that same instant, I also realized something terrible. I realized that even if I could be sure that my death would save his life, I wouldn't do it anyway. My life was more valuable to me than his.

So I emptied the bullets out of the cylinder onto the ground and threw the pistol as far as I could. It broke into parts, and John ran crazily after them trying to reassemble the pieces. Eventually, he got it to work again and fired off a round into the ground to prove it. At that point, I said, "I've had enough. If you're going to shoot yourself today, you'll have to do it alone. I'm going back to Denver." We were both emotionally spent, and he got back in the car with me.

The next day, I told John that I was returning to Cambridge. I knew I couldn't help him anymore. Sadly, we made flight arrangements, and Rita and I prepared to fly back. John came with us to the old Stapleton airport and gave me a kiss goodbye. Somehow, I felt it was like Judas kissing Jesus except reversed; I was leaving my friend to his fate. Three days later, I got a call in the middle of the night from Myron, one of John's friends from Denver. He said John got another gun, a bigger one this time, and had shot himself in the head while standing in his mother's garage. He was dead at the age of twenty-three.

I wanted to run away—to take John's money and disappear somewhere like a fugitive. I spent a sleepless night feeling like an accessory to a murder, but as the grey light of dawn appeared, I realized no one would understand what I knew, no one would recognize my responsibility, and no one would blame me for what had happened. In the end, I told John's mother I would come to the funeral in Denver. A number of John's friends came from different places. We didn't know what to do, so we tried to celebrate. Our generation had produced love-ins and a counterculture, but we hadn't learned to cry. At the service I played guitar and sang a song about love that John had written. Someone else said we should sing "Amazing Grace," so we did. The words seemed to be coming from another world but were oddly comforting.

Back in Cambridge, everything was grimly depressing and empty. I got a job driving a taxi at night in Boston and read one of John's favorite books, Heinlein's *Stranger in a Strange Land*. I thought the book was about a Jesus-like Messiah and wondered why we hadn't considered religion as a possible answer. In my taxi, I picked up some kids hitchhiking on Storrow Drive, which was not a good place to hitch a ride at night. They were in a cult called the Children of God. I looked in their eyes and realized they were terrified of the world around them. Eventually, I came to the conclusion that for me, the answer was not going to be found in Boston. It was time to leave.

I told Rita I was leaving and then hitchhiked out of town. Along the way I decided to change my name. I was going to start all over again. The desert drew me and after spending some time in Arizona, I decided to stay in Santa Fe, New Mexico. My hair grew long; my skin and Asian features were darkened by the sun. Tourists thought I was a Native American. A year or so earlier I had passed through Santa Fe and met an artist named Bill who lived in a geodesic dome outside of town. He had said then to look him up if I ever needed work and we would build an adobe house on the property he owned there. I called Bill; he said the offer was still good, so I began making bricks and lived for a while in the dome down a dirt road outside of Santa Fe.

A month or so later, I met Bob Dylan. He was looking for someone's house and knocked on what passed for a door in the metal-skinned, silver dome. He stood there wearing a purple t-shirt and a black bowler hat.

"Hey, you know where Victor lives?" he asked.

21

"Sure." I said, rising, "He's staying across the arroyo."

I walked outside with him. The songwriter and poet that I knew so well from his songs but whose life was shrouded in mystery was standing next to me. He had been called the "poet laureate of young America." His words and music had swayed my entire generation. He had torn the mask of hypocrisy off the dictates of an older world, exposing its hollow core. His words questioned all authority and led us by the thousands out of cities and suburbs onto the back roads of rebellion. Back roads became avenues; avenues became highways. With him we had rejected religion and the authority of parents, schools, and government. With him we had stepped out willingly, joyfully with raucous abandonment on a path that led away from home and all those so called leaders we regarded as mere pretenders. Everyone it seemed, including me, knew some of Dylan's songs by heart. As a teenager his words and music had played an important part in defining the reality of my youth. With him I had rejected the culture our parents embraced and built in their struggle to succeed. But I didn't know if I was freer now or if I had more difficult problems to solve than when I began.

It was not only Dylan's songs but John's death that had driven me out of Boston and compelled me to live under an assumed name, making mud bricks outside of Santa Fe. Now Bob Dylan was standing in front of me. He was lost and asking directions and without my being fully aware of it, in those few moments I lost appreciation for him as my leader. I was different. Something in me had changed. The bright New Mexico sun made us squint as I pointed out the dirt track to Victor's mobile home. I wanted to say to him, "Bob, it doesn't work. John's dead now, and we didn't find any answer 'blowin' in the wind.'" I was silent.

Bob thanked me and climbed into his light blue Ford van. It had New York plates and there was a woman, probably his then wife Sarah, in the front seat. I waved as they drove off. "Is that how heroes meet their end?" I wondered--in such ordinary circumstances? Was my earlier fascination with him like a flash flood in the desert that had run its course disappearing without a trace into the sand? Now I was more lost than ever.

CHAPTER 2

CHAPTER 2

After the chance meeting with Bob Dylan on a dirt road outside of Santa Fe I knew I was so far from home there was no point in ever trying to turn back. I had begun my life in Boston when my father was finishing up his doctoral dissertation at Harvard University. My earliest memories are of walking with my mother and sister along the banks of the Charles River near the footbridge that today connects Cambridge with the Harvard Business School on the Boston side. Later, we moved to Berkeley where my father taught Asian history at the University of California and then back to the East Coast to Virginia and Maryland when he began working for the U.S. State Department. When I was ten, my father's mentor at Harvard, Dr. Edwin Reischauer, was appointed Ambassador to Japan under President John F. Kennedy's administration. He made a request for my father to come and help him with his Japanese language and cultural expertise. We moved to Tokyo in 1961. To my young eyes modern Japanese culture was an incredible adventure. I studied Japanese as a foreign language and watched as the nation mobilized itself to succeed economically.

The drive toward prosperity through business became a primary cultural value in post-war Japan. Everything, including the family became subordinated to the goal of catching up with the West. I remember when the idea of Americans or Europeans purchasing an automobile with an obscure Japanese trade name seemed ridiculous. Even so, the Toyota Corporation thought they could persuade Westerners to buy their version of a small family car. In 1965 they brought out the first Corolla. It was not an attractive car and most Japanese could hardly pronounce the model name since it had both "R" and "L"s in it—letters that are especially difficult for the Japanese tongue to pronounce. More than forty years later, Toyota is the largest and most profitable automobile company in the world, and the Corolla is the best selling automobile of all time. Almost forty million cars bearing the Corolla name have been produced so far. I also remember when England made motorcycles. Triumph, Norton and BSA were well known and respected brands throughout the world. Actor Steve McQueen rode a Triumph in the 1960s classic movie *The Great Escape*. In that same decade, another almost unknown Japanese company introduced a 50cc motorized scooter with a plastic front called the Super Cub. Soon Honda and its Japanese competitors, Yamaha, Kawasaki and Suzuki dominated the entire motorcycle industry. Now, English-made motorcycles are mostly out of production and some are considered collector's items. These and countless other examples demonstrated the power of culture to focus the efforts of an entire people on economic or other goals.

When I graduated from the American School in Japan in Tokyo, I was accepted for freshman admission at Tufts University in Medford, Massachusetts near Boston. The university showed me that American culture had reached and passed a breaking point. Once, in a period of intellectual despair, I asked some of my professors if there was such a thing as truth. None of them seemed to believe there was an absolute reference point for anything in the world. I wandered through nearby Harvard Square and gazed at the seal of the university where my father had studied and earned his doctorate. "*Veritas*" it said, "Truth." Somehow I knew deep down that something had to be true for anything to be true. If there really was no "veritas," then we were all doomed.

As a freshman at Tufts, I met my friend John, whose death changed the course of my life, and I also met Rita, who shares this part of my story and who later became my wife. When I ended up in Santa Fe with no money, no future, and nothing much to show for more than two decades of life on the planet, she came to stay with me. One cold winter day in New Mexico, Rita was picked up hitchhiking by a woman in a little blue Volkswagen with bumper stickers on the back that read, "Jesus Died For Your Sins" and "Guess Who's Coming Again?" A month or so earlier, Rita had gone alone to Santa Fe's only synagogue on *Yom Kippur*, the Jewish Day of Atonement. It was not just because of her Jewish upbringing, but in her own confused state she was reaching out to God. Although she did not have the encounter with God she was seeking that day, it was a memorable service because someone ran in to announce that Israel had been attacked. The Yom Kippur War had begun. So when she entered Abbie Brown's car, Rita asked her, "Is he really coming?" Abbie said something like, "Of course He's coming." She proceeded to tell Rita about all the prophecies in the Bible concerning Israel, how they were relevant to today and the soon return of the Messiah, and that there were still other prophecies that had not been fulfilled. Abbie impressed Rita so much that they began a friendship and later Rita agreed to attend a meeting at a local coffee house called "Shalom."

The night Rita went to "Shalom" she was supposed to meet me in the bar of a well-known Santa Fe hotel. She called several times and asked the front desk to page me. I would have told her to get out of that place and to stay away from religious freaks, but I never heard anyone calling for me and went home early. That night, Rita listened to a young man named Andrew tell his story. He was a Jew from California and had originally come out with his young wife Connie and some friends to start a commune high in the hills of northern New Mexico. They wanted to launch a new society based on pure values away from the corruption of modern civilization. Living without electricity and running water and plowing rocky, odd-shaped fields with horses and hand-made tools when their first son was born, they named him Rainbow.

Yet, somehow along the way it had all gone wrong. At one point, they tried to befriend a young drifter who came by. When Andrew was away from the commune one day, the drifter took a rifle that was kept in the house, murdered another member of the community, and disappeared. They were stunned by this act of senseless evil and wondered how the intended beauty of their lifestyle which was so close to nature had become so permanently darkened. Some months later, a few hippies hiked into their remote community, shared the story of their faith in Jesus, and Andrew, along with some of the others, believed.

As Rita listened to Andrew tell his story, she was struck by his resemblance to our friend John. Afterwards, some of the women asked if they could pray for Rita. She refused at first but then allowed them to pray. In the process, something inside Rita broke. She began to weep, and a deep spiritual change began within her. When she returned to where we lived, I knew in less than twenty-four hours that she was different. She had found hope. Something new was alive in her heart.

When I asked Rita why she seemed so different, she couldn't clearly describe all that had taken place. She did manage to say it was about Jesus and the people had Bibles. My heart sank. I figured I had tried that as a child, and it didn't work. But I couldn't deny the reality of Rita's new-found faith. She wanted me to meet her new friends. I was hesitant at first and then agreed.

It was December, and I was now working as an auto mechanic because adobe bricks made outside after the first frosts are too crumbly for use. Rita arranged a meeting with some of her new friends, one of whom was a mechanic like me. They invited us for a family-style Christmas Eve dinner. I had a lot of questions about what they believed, but after the meal a strange feeling came over me. I looked down at my hands. They were rough and deeply stained by automobile oil and grease. My clothes were worn, my hair long and matted. Suddenly, I felt a deep inner sadness. How had I ended up here using a false name, fixing cars, and living on a few dollars a day? Was this what I was born to do? Was this my life's real purpose? What was I doing here?

"Do you want to pray with us?" they were asking me as we sat around the fireplace. "Why not?" I thought. They led me in a prayer. I invited Jesus into my life. Afterwards, nothing seemed to have happened. I overheard them whispering, "He's not ready to make a real commitment." So they told me, "Listen, God is a Spirit, and those who worship Him have to worship Him in Spirit and truth." I didn't know that they were quoting from the New Testament, but it seemed to make sense. My psychedelic drug experiences had convinced me that the spirit world was real, except that most of the spirits I had met while on drugs were ugly or terrifying.

I wanted to know, "If God is a Spirit, what is He like?"

"His Spirit is just like Jesus," they said.

Knowing that Jesus was a good man who didn't advocate violence, I asked, "Okay, how do I meet this spirit?"

"Just read the New Testament and go out somewhere alone and talk to God."

With a skeptical satisfaction mixed with suspicion, I asked, "That's it? You don't want me to join anything or sign anything or do anything weird? This means I don't really need you either, right?"

"That's right. It's just you and God!"

"Okay, I can do that."

And so in the days that followed I started walking out into the desert and began talking to God. At first it was strange, but soon it felt more natural. Then on the third or fourth day it began to happen. I felt the presence of someone else there with me. I knew it was the Spirit of God. It felt clean, refreshing, and unlike the dark, threatening spiritual experiences I had been used to. I started to enjoy being in the presence of this Spirit. I wanted to go back to the people we had met and tell them what they had told me to do had worked!

When I met Rita's new friends again, I wanted to know more about Jesus. I knew now that only God could answer the questions I had. The psychiatrist I had visited while still back in Boston had wanted to focus on my feelings of pain and guilt. He thought if he could change my feelings about what I had been through, everything would be all right. Inside I knew that I carried a real, moral responsibility along with John for his decisions and that it wasn't just about my feelings. From my conversations with the psychiatrist I had concluded that only someone like God could understand my responsibility. Only God had the right to determine the degree of my guilt. Only God could forgive me.

"Well, Jesus died for your sins," our friends said. "God so loved the world that He gave His only Son so that whoever believes in him will not die but have everlasting life."

"Are you telling me that Jesus *on purpose* gave up his life for me?"

"Yes. If you were the only person on earth, He still would have sacrificed Himself."

The thought intrigued me. Could there be someone who would deliberately make a decision to give up his life for someone else and then resolutely carry out the plan? Was there someone alive who valued the life of his friends more than he valued his own? Whoever that person might be, I knew sadly that it wasn't me. I had discovered that my own life was more precious to me than the life of my best friend. Now I felt like I needed to know this person Jesus.

A year or so earlier, if someone had said that I was the object of God's love and that His only Son Jesus had died for me, I would have said, "What for? I didn't ask Him to die for me. What a waste!" But now, after John's death I had to know if this story was true. I started to read the New Testament searching for clues that it was more than a good story, more than a collection of religious myths. Was this Jesus real?

One day, while reading the gospel of John, I came to the part in chapter ten where Jesus is proclaiming the source of his authority to his legalistic, religious adversaries. Finally, He says to them, "I and the Father are one." At the moment I read those six words, it was as if a hole opened up in the page, and I was looking into Jesus' life. All at once I knew that He knew me and every other man on the face of the earth. He knew that our issues are always with our fathers. He knew that my father was a good man who loved me but wasn't emotionally equipped to express it very well. My father gave me everything materially that he possibly could but retreated from offering his deepest feelings. I struggled with the distance I felt and later just came to accept it as a fact of life.

But deep inside I was angry. As a child in the Episcopalian church I had been taught that God was a lot like my father. Good, but distant—not connected to the realities of my personal life. Over the years I became at first scornful and then indignant at the idea of God, our Creator and Supreme Authority being distant and unapproachable. Especially after my friend's death, I thought, "If God is somewhere far away, busy with his own divine things, why am I supposed to honor or worship Him? I am down here on earth struggling with complicated and ugly human issues. Where's the connection?"

However, when I read that single verse in the gospel of John, in one revelatory instant I understood clearly that Jesus was truly human. He understood how important a father is to every man. His strength came from his relationship with his own father. Jesus was real, what he said was true, and that meant God was not distant but here with us. I also realized at that moment that I believed in Him for the first time. I knelt on the dirt floor of the wooden pump-house where I was living and prayed my first real prayer of consecration, "Lord, take me as your servant and let your light shine through me." This time I felt the prayer coming from the core of my being, and I knew in that same inner place that God's Spirit was somehow close by and that He had heard my cry.

When I went back to my friends, I asked, "So, where is Jesus now?" "He's in heaven with God, his Father," my friends said, "He's alive from the dead and rules God's kingdom through His Spirit." I learned that Jesus is no longer a suffering servant but a reigning King and that being a believer was about learning to be a part of His kingdom. It meant learning to trust Him and accepting His rule in every area of my life. I thought I knew what it meant to be a citizen of a democratic country, but I had never lived in a kingdom before. What did it mean to serve a king? This was going to be something new.

CHAPTER 3

CHAPTER 3

I began to read the Bible whenever I had a chance. My new friends said it was inspired by God's Spirit. At first it seemed strange to be reading about events and issues that took place so long ago, but soon I began to grasp that it is basically all about God and His kingdom. I learned that God's kingdom is simply the realm in which God rules as King. It may be in your heart, your family or community, or a Messianic age coming in the future, but God's kingdom is found at anytime and anywhere He rules as King.

It was immediately clear to me that God's reign as King was His intention from the time of creation. The Bible describes God as the Creator of the universe and of our world. When He made the first humans, they were created to be like Him and made to rule over the rest of creation. As I read the Bible, I saw that the kingdom of God was the focal point of Jesus' ministry. According to Matthew's gospel He began His work with the proclamation, "Repent, for the kingdom of heaven is at hand!" (Matthew 4:17). Matthew's intended audience was mostly Jews, so he usually used the term "kingdom of heaven" in place of "kingdom of God" because religious Jews, even to this day, consider God's name too holy to pronounce. Jesus' method of teaching included the frequent use of parables. Many of them begin with the words, "the kingdom of heaven is like…" followed by His illustration. In Matthew chapter thirteen there are six such parables all beginning in the same way. In the well-known Lord's Prayer, Jesus taught His disciples to pray for the coming of God's kingdom to the earth (Matthew 6:10) and later; in the same Sermon on the Mount, He instructed His disciples to seek for God's kingdom before all other things (Matthew 6:33).

When Jesus began His ministry in the Galilee, the message of God's kingdom was His principal teaching, and this message was reinforced by His ability to work miracles of healing. Matthew recorded that "Jesus was going throughout all Galilee, teaching in their synagogues and proclaiming the gospel of the kingdom, and healing every kind of disease and every kind of sickness among the people" (Matthew 4:23). Jesus came to inaugurate a new covenant between Israel and God, but the concept of God's rule as King was not foreign to the people of Israel. The Jewish followers of Jesus understood that God's kingdom, that is, His rightful rule of their nation, was uniquely part of Israel's heritage, and they hoped it would be a reality again in their own time.

As I studied the Bible, I began to realize that as a non-Jew, I had, through faith in Jesus, become a "son of Abraham

42

(Galatians 3:7) and been "grafted into the olive tree" of Israel (Romans 11:17). Now, I was sharing in Israel's history and heritage! I learned that before the centuries of captivity in Egypt the people of Israel were a close-knit family group led by a lineage of patriarchs chosen by God: first Abraham, then Isaac followed by Jacob, whose name was changed to Israel. It was one of Jacob's sons, Joseph who led the entire family (the Bible says about seventy people) to Egypt for refuge. After the deaths of Joseph and the Pharaoh who befriended him, the people of Israel became slaves of the Egyptians for 400 years. As slaves they grew into a people group roughly divided into the twelve tribes of their patriarchs. At the time of the Exodus, the men of Israel numbered in the hundreds of thousands (Exodus 12:37); some say they were as many as three or four million people including women and children, but they were not a nation as we know it. They had been slaves for centuries and had no national infrastructure or consciousness. They had never had a land of their own and at that stage, without a government, legal system or national culture, they would surely have been classified as dysfunctional in terms of nationhood. However, after the deliverance from Egypt, under the leadership of the prophet Moses, God met them in the desert and made a divine covenant with the people of Israel. Through that covenant, for the first time, they became a nation and God became their King. Thus, Israel is portrayed in the Bible as a prototype, an early picture of the kingdom of God on earth. Here is what

43

God spoke to the people of Israel through Moses:

Now then, if you will indeed obey My voice and keep My covenant, then you shall be My own possession among all the peoples, for all the earth is Mine; and you shall be to Me a kingdom of priests and a holy nation. These are the words that you shall speak to the sons of Israel. (Exodus 19:5-6)

Somehow, I had it in my mind that Moses was king of Israel, but I learned that was never the case. He was called to be God's prophet the servant of the Lord. God said, "You shall be to *Me* a kingdom of priests and a holy nation." So God Himself became King of Israel and there in the desert, He began forming the extended family of Abraham through Isaac and Jacob into a nation for the first time. Becoming God's kingdom of priests meant that Israel's role as a nation was to serve all other nations and to be their example.

Years later, after entering the land that God had promised, Israel was led by judges and later by the prophet Samuel. At that time, the people of Israel became secure in their own land and began being envious of the nations around them. Perhaps it was embarrassing to have no capital city, no royal palace, no honor guard, and no human king to impress the foreign visitors. They must have wondered, "Why do we have to be so different from everyone else? Other nations have a physical

44

supreme leader or at least the image of a god in their temples; our God and King is invisible!" According to the Bible, the people of Israel complained to Samuel and demanded that he ask God to give them a human king. Because of their desire to be like other nations, the people of Israel rejected God's kingdom.

> *But the thing was displeasing in the sight of Samuel when they said, "Give us a king to judge us" and Samuel prayed to the LORD. The LORD said to Samuel, "Listen to the voice of the people in regard to all that they say to you, for they have not rejected you, but they have rejected Me from being king over them.* (1Samuel 8:4-7)

It is clear that having a human king as the sole and sovereign ruler of Israel was never God's design. In God's plan, human kings were meant to rule on His behalf. In the years that followed there were many men who ruled over God's people, but only one of them was ever known as a truly great king. David, the second king of Israel, was superior to all the other kings because he saw himself as a small king compared to God, who was always the greater King. In his psalms, David repeatedly refers to God as his King, and he considered himself subject to God's laws. When David's warriors fought their way into Bethlehem to get him a drink of water from the well he had known as a child, David poured the water out as an offering to God. He declared that only God was worthy of his men's sacrifice. David was called a man "after God's own heart."

Sadly, after David, the people of Israel were increasingly ruled by kings who led them away from worship of the true God and away from obedience to His laws. David's son Solomon eventually turned from following the Lord and after him, the kingdom was divided by civil war with ten tribes in the north and two in the south. In the northern kingdom, called Israel, there was never a good king. One evil king followed another and idolatry, corruption, political intrigue and murder became rampant. In 722 B.C., the weakened northern kingdom was conquered by the Assyrians and the people taken into captivity. The southern kingdom, known as Judah, had a few good kings who actively sought reform, but there were many bad ones, and in 586 B.C. their Babylonian enemies overcame them. Israel as God's nation and the example of His kingdom on earth was destroyed and the people taken into captivity. This was because of the failure of human kings to rule the nation according to God's plan and His Law. God's outrage and sorrow over the plight of His people is evident in the words of the prophet Ezekiel who prophesied from captivity in Babylon;

"What you have in your mind shall never be, when you say, 'We will be like the Gentiles, like the families in other countries, serving wood and stone.' As I live," says the Lord GOD, *"surely with a mighty hand, with an*

outstretched arm, and with fury poured out, I will rule over you." (Ezekiel 20:32-34)

After seventy years, a remnant of the southern tribes returned to the land of Israel under Nehemiah and Ezra. The walls of Jerusalem were rebuilt and a small temple reconstructed. This was not really a triumphant return. Only a few of the survivors from the southern kingdom returned. Some of the older people who remembered the glory of the earlier temple wept in disappointment when they saw the foundations of the new temple (Ezra 3:12). In the years that followed, the nation was never completely free again, except for a short period under the Hasmoneans. They were under the Persians, then the Greeks, and finally the Romans dominated the region. Israel was a small, unimportant nation under the rule of great empires. During the centuries between the Old and the New Testaments there was no prophetic voice in Israel, and the Jewish people longed for a visitation from God as in the earlier days of their history. I am sure that many in Israel prayed to God during this time and repented for their forefathers' decision to follow human kings. It was at this spiritual and political low point, a voice was heard crying in the wilderness "Prepare the way of the Lord!" John the Baptist came to herald the coming of someone greater than he. Then Jesus appeared in the power of the Holy Spirit preaching "Repent, for the kingdom of God is at hand!" and teaching the principles of the

47

kingdom of God. His ministry was accompanied by unusual miracles and He was welcomed by many in Israel as a great prophet, a possible deliverer and, by some as the Messiah.

I know that many Christians today regard Jesus' message about the kingdom of God as a completely New Testament concept. However, I came to see that nothing could be further from the truth. If you believe that the Bible's teaching about God's kingdom begins in the New Testament, it is like coming into a long movie only after the intermission! You can find out how the story ends, but you will never understand why it ends that way. You will learn who are the main characters in the story but never really understand their motivations. Jewish people of Jesus' day understood the concept of God's rule as King. They knew from the Scriptures and the history of their own nation that God had once been their King, and they longed for His rule to be restored. The Jewish understanding was then, and still is today, that the Messiah will come from God and rule Israel as King. This belief was deep in the hearts of Jesus' own disciples throughout their years with Him and even after His resurrection from the dead.

Imagine if you were given five minutes alone with the Lord Himself. What a privilege that would be, and what if you could ask Him one question during that meeting? What would you ask Him? It would have to be a very important question! The disciples' understanding of God's kingdom is revealed in the question they asked in their last five minutes with Jesus before

His ascension into heaven in Acts 1:6: "So when they had come together, they were asking Him, saying, "Lord, is it at this time You are restoring the kingdom to Israel?" The disciples asked Jesus when He was going to restore God's kingdom, that is, to bring God's rule back to their nation.

Many Christians wonder why the disciples asked the Lord such a strange question. Didn't they realize by then that God's kingdom is spiritual, not earthly and for all nations not just theirs? Were they carnally nationalistic or just not thinking? However, the reason we may not understand the importance of this question is because we have come into the "movie" after the intermission! God's kingdom has always been about establishing His rule on earth. Moreover, since the Exodus from Egypt, in obedience as a shining light and in disobedience as an object of sorrow, Israel was God's example of His intended and lawful reign over every area of society and culture.

Jesus replied to His disciples, "It is not for you to know times or epochs which the Father has fixed by His own authority; but you will receive power when the Holy Spirit has come upon you; and you shall be My witnesses both in Jerusalem, and in all Judea and Samaria, and even to the remotest part of the earth" (Acts 1:7-8). He did not deny that the kingdom of God would be restored to Israel, but He deliberately avoided saying when. Jesus knew His disciples expected God's kingdom to appear immediately (Luke 19:11). If He had said it would take more than 2,000 years, they would have been confused

49

and discouraged. Instead Jesus directed their attention to the power of the Holy Spirit to be a "witness" of the kingdom, not only locally but also throughout the world.

It is obvious to me now that Jesus was teaching them that the kingdom of God would, from that time on, include all nations. It would not be limited to Israel and the task of reaching the world would take centuries. Bringing the transforming power of God's kingdom into every culture requires more than miracles of healing. It takes supernatural power from God's Spirit to make the life of each believer a witness that testifies to the sovereign rule of God. Developing a character and lifestyle that points to God is a process that starts in the heart of each disciple and extends outward into the culture of each nation. Jesus was prophesying the spread of the culture transforming gospel of the kingdom throughout the world and saying that it would eventually return to the nation of Israel, as it is now through the present day lives and witness of Jews who honor Him as King.

I could see that Jesus' disciples' understanding of God's kingdom was correctly focused on the culture and society of Israel. These men and their contemporaries were not ignorant of God's word and His purposes. They knew more about the Lord's personal life than we will ever know, and some of them were directly inspired by Him to write the gospels. We know that the divine inspiration in the words of the New Testament is always in what the authors understood from God rather than in how we, centuries later, interpret what they wrote. Therefore, our modern understanding of the kingdom of God must be rooted, as theirs was, in the reality of Israel as God's chosen nation. I began to see Israel of the Bible as the picture, prototype, and example of what God wants and what He does not want among all societies on this earth. The most important question for me, therefore, became "How did God rule Israel then and how does He rule my life in His kingdom today?"

CHAPTER 4

CHAPTER 4

It wasn't easy making the transition from life as an unbeliever to my new spiritual home in the culture of God's kingdom. There seemed to be a myriad of things to learn. There were moments of despair when I considered giving up, and there were times of intense joy when it seemed like the presence of God was so real that it was almost physical. I learned God's kingdom could be found inside of me, in my thoughts and motives, or revealed through the people around me. Nevertheless, I struggled with God's authority. I had grown up influenced by movie stars like James Dean, comedians like Lenny Bruce, and musicians like Jimi Hendrix and Janis Joplin. They were heroes because they were talented rebels, and they all died young. Now I started to learn from the Bible that rebellion against God is called sin and that sin results in death. It was a startling revelation. The problem was that I was drawn to rebellion. Something in me responded positively to it. Rebellion was in me. But now, God's reign was in me too. In a very short time I became aware that there was a war going on inside my soul.

Soon after I started to believe in Jesus, Rita and I were invited to a New Year's Eve prayer and worship service at a local church. I wanted to go, but my employer at the garage was throwing a New Year's party, and I also wanted to be there. We decided to go to both. At the party, liquor flowed freely, hashish was being smoked, and everyone was having a good time. I brought my guitar to play some music, but as midnight approached Rita started saying it was time to go. After a while she got her coat and left the party. I was torn between staying and leaving and upset with Rita's abrupt decision. I followed her out into the cold night where new snow was lightly falling. "Why do we have to leave now?" I wanted to know. "Because the service is starting soon, and if we walk there now we will just make it," she said. "I feel like staying," I said, trying to persuade her. "Okay, then I will go alone," Rita said as she started to walk away.

I knew it was a crucial turning point. It was more than just about a party or a church service. I could either go on with my new faith or go back to where I had been. The choice was mine. I knew what I had to do, but it hurt to make the decision. "All right, I'll go too!" I said and slammed my guitar case down onto the snowy ground so hard that later I found out the instrument was cracked. I caught up with Rita and together we went to the church.

Inside, we sat among a few dozen strangers and started to sing what they called "praise songs." They were songs about

Jesus and God put to major key melodies, and they sounded to me like nursery rhymes. We had grown up with popular music that changed the entire world and considered ourselves young *afficionados* of modern rock music who could barely listen to AM radio "bubble gum" commercial pop songs. Rita had gone to Woodstock and walked miles through the mud because of the music our generation loved. Now we were singing simple, three chord songs with everyone else, swinging our legs like kids from the wooden pew unable to stop smiling at the people around us. The little church was God's house that night, and we were welcomed in it.

In a short time we began attending Bible studies at "Shalom" and other meetings whenever we could. We began learning about the books that make up the Bible as well as a new kind of language used by the people in the "fellowship." They often quoted Bible verses or parts of verses integrated into normal sentences. They prayed before each meal, even in restaurants, and everyone had their own story or "testimony." The people were from all kinds of backgrounds. There were scientists from the research facilities in nearby Los Alamos, where during World War II the American atomic bomb was designed. There were homeless people, single mothers, local people with Hispanic names and hippies like us. It seemed like every time I sat down with someone and asked them, "How did you come to the Lord?" an incredible story would come forth. Some people had been through so much pain in their lives it made our own struggles seem small and insignificant. I realized I was looking at a cross section of American society that most people like me only experienced by watching movies.

In February, the little "Shalom" fellowship took a group of us out of Santa Fe to a place in the mountains called "Glorieta." It was so cold that there was ice on the Pecos River when we got there. The reason for our visit was for me to be baptized. I read in the Bible that this was for believers, and it meant my old rebellious nature was supposed to die and be buried and that because of faith, I was going to "rise" like Jesus did from the dead to live a new life. There were a few others being baptized also that day, and I looked at them as if they were like the martyrs I had read about from ancient times. We were all giving up our lives to God. It felt scary and thrilling. People sang and prayers were prayed. When my turn came and the icy water closed in over my head, I felt something deep within me was forever restructured. I thought back to the sprinkling I saw babies receive in the Episcopalian Church when I was growing up. It seemed to have no relationship to the stark reality of what I had just experienced.

One evening, Don Compton, the leader of "Shalom," said that everyone was going to his father-in-law's church to be "baptized in the Holy Spirit." I didn't know what that meant, but since I thought it sounded exciting, I went. That night at a little Pentecostal church that was literally across the railroad tracks in Albuquerque we heard Reverend Smith preach about the

58

Holy Spirit. He said it was the same power from God that raised Jesus from the dead and that the Holy Spirit was meant to live inside each of us. We were to be His "temple" and the result of Him coming inside of us was that we would speak in "tongues." I learned that tongues were words I didn't comprehend with my mind, but they were a communication from the Spirit inside of me with God. At the end of his message, the pastor invited us to come forward for prayer. We went up to the front; he put his hand on my head, and I began to speak in tongues. It was a strange and uplifting feeling. My eyes were closed, and I began to see a bright blue heaven with some clouds and the sun shining through. As I continued to pray in tongues, it was as if I was lifted up into heaven! After a few minutes, it was over, and we went back to our seats. However, after that I continued privately to use the new language I had received.

Now that I was a believer, I was filled with a deep restlessness and dissatisfaction with my inability to curb my own impulses and appetites. I wanted to serve God, but I didn't know where to start. I knew I needed discipline in my life and decided to join the military. I hitchhiked down to Albuquerque and took an aptitude test at a local Navy recruiting station. They asked me what I wanted to do and I said, "Submarines." The recruiting officer said he'd never had someone score that high on the test at that station and told me I could sign up for six years if I was ready to leave later that week. I wanted to go, but said I'd have to check with my "family," meaning Rita and my friends at Shalom. When I asked them the next day, the older guys there laughed and said, "That's not God's will for your life!" However, they too knew I needed discipline, and so it was decided I would be sent to serve the Lord somewhere.

Somewhere turned out to be an outreach to the Navajo people near a little town called Crown Point in western New Mexico. Brother Everly and his wife lived in a mobile home in this desert location, and my job was to help them with whatever was needed. When I arrived, Brother Everly showed me his library of Christian books, and I borrowed a booklet by a man named Franklin Hall. It was called *Fasting: Atomic Power With God*. As I read this small book, I became convinced it was God's will for me to discipline and purify myself with a forty-day fast. I moved into a small trailer on their property and began drinking only water a few times a day. My duties with the Everlys were light; several times a week I had to water the trees around the trailers and on Sunday drive a van to pick up all the Navajo women who were attending services in the small chapel. Most days I would get up in the morning, read the Bible, and climb up on the mesa to pray.

At first, I experienced headaches, nausea and dizziness, but by the third or fourth day I was no longer hungry at all. I began to have a mental clarity that I had never before experienced. I felt able to concentrate on a single thought or passage from the Bible for hours at a time. It seemed like I was being purged and purified of all the darkness in my previous life. After a while I felt sorry for the others who were eating meals and carrying on their lives as usual. Rita came to visit and began fasting with me. The arid desert landscape made us think about the land of the Bible, and we were sensing strongly that somehow Israel was in our future. We prayed together a lot, and it seemed God's presence and the inner voice of His Spirit were close at hand. It was clear our destinies were bound together in a plan God was beginning to reveal. We decided God was telling us we should get married.

After three weeks, Rita stopped fasting and returned to Santa Fe, but I continued because I had promised God I would complete the forty days. One morning, however, on the thirty-second or thirty-third day, I went up on the mesa as usual, but then I had a distinct and clear impression that I should go down and join Brother Everly for breakfast. When I entered the trailer, he was frying eggs. I sat down and said, "I think God is telling me my fast is over." "Okay, fine," he said, and so I made a cup of tea with sugar in it and started to drink.

I know now that it was the voice of God telling me to break my fast, but then I couldn't discern between God's voice, the voice of my own soul, or the voice of an evil spirit. As soon as I began to drink the tea, a powerful sense of condemnation came over me, and I felt I had failed God and broken my promise to fast the entire forty days. Not knowing what to do, I left the tea unfinished and went back up on the mesa. A day or so later, I returned to Santa Fe but for the final seven or eight days of the fast, I "punished" myself by wetting my mouth with water and only allowing a small amount to trickle down my throat. By the time I tried to break the fast after the fortieth day, I was so dehydrated, I couldn't swallow anything, and my friends rushed me to the hospital.

At first, the doctors and nurses were not sure I would survive the night. There was so little liquid in my body they could not find a vein in which to insert a needle to drip nutrients into my blood stream. Finally, they did succeed, and in a day or so I bounced back to health. During my three days in the hospital I felt an indescribable peace and an exhilarating joy that sometimes was like an "out of the body" experience. It was a Catholic hospital and on the wall across from my bed there hung a crucifix. I stared at that image of Jesus for hours and wondered how He had endured such punishment without breaking and begging to be taken down from the cross.

In the bed next to me was a Hispanic man. He was middle-aged and apparently dying. His body was hooked up to many tubes and wires that were connected to beeping medical devices. His wife and children came in to sit by his bed and cry. On the day I was to be released, I had been invited to attend a dinner hosted by the local Full Gospel Businessmen of Santa Fe. I knew that they regularly prayed for the sick, so I told the family that I would take the man's name to the dinner and ask them to pray. That evening, I handed a note with his name on it to the leaders and everyone prayed. The following day,

I returned to the hospital to pick up the bill for my stay and went back to the ward. Incredibly, the man was sitting up in bed, the tubes and wires were gone and the family was ecstatic. "What did you do?" they wanted to know. "Nothing," I said, "we just prayed." He had been in the Marines, so I gave him a little pamphlet I had about the toughness of God's love and left feeling very happy. Was this the normal life of a believer?

In the months that followed, Rita and I pursued our plans to be married. Although we had known each other for more than four years, we had never thought a permanent relationship was possible. Human love was just too weak and unpredictable, but now we knew the reality of God's unchanging love. We also were learning that God's character is one of uncommon faithfulness. Our faith in Him was really a response to His faithfulness in creating and caring for us. We learned that God relates to His human creation through covenants which are unbreakable agreements that He fiercely protects. Unexpectedly, we discovered a foundation of love and faithfulness had been given to us. We could make promises to each other and expect God to help us keep them. So we talked with others in our small fellowship, and everyone seemed to be in favor of our decision.

Our choices, however, were extremely difficult for our parents to accept. All they knew is that we had been rebellious, even self-destructive, and now may have become caught up in a religious cult of some kind. Although none of our parents had met either intended spouse, we were now inviting them to come to a wedding in remote Santa Fe, a tiny city in the mountains of northern New Mexico. Nevertheless, in a time of private prayer I had a "vision" and saw a wedding ceremony with all our parents not only present but participating and reading from the Bible with us. I didn't know then that it would take another year for this to happen. What we were doing was so far removed from Rita's parents' expectations of her that when we pressed on with our plans to marry, they declined our invitation. My parents were still living in Japan, and because my father had work commitments, only my mother was able to attend by volunteering to chaperone a flight of Korean orphans to the United States. Rita's uncle and aunt came from California, and my sister flew out from New York. We had a wonderful but simple ceremony followed by a reception in one of Santa Fe's public parks. I remember the intense joy of the day as we celebrated outdoors while the sun went down behind the Sangre de Cristo (Spanish for "Blood of Christ") mountains ringing Santa Fe, a city whose name means "Holy Faith."

I looked at the people around us that day, former hippies like Andrew and his wife, Connie, a few college friends from Boston, Jim, the brother of my friend John who had died, Abbie who had first taken Rita to "Shalom," others from Santa Fe, and a lone hitchhiker we had picked up earlier that day and invited to the wedding. I marveled at the faithfulness of God to bring Rita and me out of our previous lives which were so marked by darkness and futility. We were in a new place now beginning new lives and surrounded by new friends. Not only were we being changed, but we had entered an entirely different culture of faith and hope that was based on eternal love.

CHAPTER 5

CHAPTER 5

It didn't take long for me to learn that the culture of God's kingdom is first and foremost a lawful culture. God's laws for Israel were an integral part of a covenant He made with them as a nation. This covenant was in the form of a contract. God limited Himself by promising to act toward His people in a loving, just and predictable way. In exchange, He made demands of the people including the requirement of obedience to the laws He laid down in the covenant. According to the Bible, the people of Israel accepted the covenant God offered to them while still an unformed nation in the Sinai desert.

> *So Moses came and called the elders of the people, and set before them all these words which the LORD had commanded him. All the people answered together and said, "All that the LORD has spoken we will do!" And Moses brought back the words of the people to the LORD.* (Exodus 19:7-8)

The laws that God gave Israel through the prophet Moses are written in the first five books of the Bible. We call these books from Genesis to Deuteronomy the Pentateuch, or the five Books of Moses. In the New Testament they are often referred to as "the Law," and in Judaism they are known as the *Torah*. According to Jewish tradition there are 613 commandments found in the Torah. Lists of these commandments today are readily available on the Internet. Religious Jews study these laws throughout their lives and, through the interpretation of commentaries contained in the *Talmud*, seek to obey them as literally as possible.

As a child, before we moved to Japan, I had lived in Montgomery County, Maryland near Washington D. C. where almost all of my friends were Jewish. On Wednesdays after school there was no one to play with because they were all required by their parents to attend Hebrew classes. In the fall, on Yom Kippur, the Day of Atonement, my elementary school would be almost deserted because everyone was at home fasting with their families. The boys I knew were all looking forward to their *Bar Mitzvah* ceremonies which would take place when they were thirteen. Now, years later, it was obvious to me that Jesus and all his disciples were also Jews. The only Bible they knew was the *Tenach* (a Hebrew acronym from the words: Torah, Prophets, and Writings) or what Christians call the Old Testament. For thousands of years, religious Jews have regarded the Torah as God's Law. I saw that a major theme

70

throughout the four gospels is the conflict between the legalism of the religious Jewish Pharisees and the disciplined freedom of Jesus' life and teaching.

In religious Judaism, it is anticipated that the Messiah will come as King of Israel. He will be greater than all other Jewish leaders, give the correct interpretation of God's Law and judge all mankind. As I studied the Bible, I quickly saw that the reason the religious leaders of Jesus' day accused Him of breaking God's laws was their failure to recognize Him as Messiah and King. However, I also began to see that many Christians believe that Jesus is their Savior and consider Him to be their "best friend" or "older brother" but fail to honor Him as a King who expects His commands to be obeyed. It seems that many people consider Jesus' teachings to be "spiritual guidelines" or good advice. It is as if we read the words of Jesus in the New Testament that say, "A new commandment I give to you..." and subtly interpret them to mean, "A new proposal I submit for your consideration..."

I was now realizing that lawlessness in the New Testament is a serious offense that strikes directly at the foundations of God's kingdom. Jesus taught His disciples that the days preceding His return would be marked by an increase in *anomia*, which I learned is New Testament Greek for lawlessness. In the *Septuagint*, the Greek language Old Testament used by some of the New Testament writers, the word used for Torah, or law, is *nomos* from which the word *anomia* (lawlessness) is derived.

In Matthew chapter twenty-four, Jesus gave a description of the times before His return. Jesus said, "Because lawlessness (anomia) is increased, most people's love will grow cold" (Matthew 24:12). Jesus didn't say that people's love in the end times would grow cold for lack of kindness or mercy from God. Jesus taught that people who have some love for God will lose it because they are not sufficiently protected by the structure of divine law. When he wrote about the end times, the apostle Paul described the world leader called the Antichrist as the man of anomia, or "lawlessness" (2Thessalonians 2:3). He wrote that Jesus' return will not occur before the Antichrist is revealed. Paul did not write that the Antichrist would be characterized by brutality, deception, or violence. He wrote that the Antichrist will be a man who embodies rejection of God's lawful reign and that the "mystery of lawlessness is already at work" (2Thessalonians 2:7).

Those who consider themselves followers of Jesus will not be immune from practicing lawlessness. Jesus made this clear when He said:

> *Not everyone who says to Me, "Lord, Lord," will enter the kingdom of heaven, but he who does the will of My Father who is in heaven will enter. Many will say to Me on that day, "Lord, Lord, did we not prophesy in Your name, and in Your name cast out demons, and in Your name perform many miracles?" And then I will declare*

72

to them, "I never knew you; depart from Me, you who
practice lawlessness [anomia]." (Matthew 7:21-23)

From this, I saw that according to Jesus, a primary
requirement for entry into His kingdom is acceptance of His
law. Rejection of God's lawful reign will prevent entry into
God's kingdom even for those who believe in God and try to
serve Him. The abilities to work miracles and to prophesy are
not the ultimate sign of acceptance by God. Living under God's
reign is what it means to be known by God in His kingdom.
According to Jesus' disciple John, lawlessness is another word
for sin. He wrote, "Everyone who practices sin also practices
lawlessness; and sin is lawlessness" (1John 3:4). If lawlessness
is another word for sin, then righteousness would be a way of
describing life under God's lawful reign.

I was finding the Bible increasingly fascinating, and I
was drawn into reading it as much as I could. A friend gave
me a leather-bound study Bible called a "Thompson Chain
Reference" and told me to use colored marking pens to help
my study. These studies led me repeatedly to a part of the New
Testament that many consider Jesus' most important teaching:
the "Sermon on the Mount," which begins in Matthew chapter
five. There is an interesting parallel in the Bible between what
is written in Exodus chapters nineteen and twenty and in the
New Testament gospel of Matthew chapters four and five. In
Exodus chapter nineteen, God met Israel in the desert and

chose the twelve tribes as His covenant nation. In the following chapter, God called His servant, the prophet Moses, up to the mountain and gave him the Law for the nation of Israel. In Matthew chapter four, Jesus chose his twelve Jewish disciples who were clearly meant to represent a new, redeemed people of Israel. In Matthew chapter five, Jesus calls the chosen twelve up to a mountain in the Galilee and gives them the law of His kingdom. He directly addressed the issue of God's kingdom and Torah in His most famous sermon. He said:

> *Do not think that I came to abolish the Law or the Prophets; I did not come to abolish but to fulfill. For truly I say to you, until heaven and earth pass away, not the smallest letter or stroke shall pass from the Law until all is accomplished. Whoever then annuls one of the least of these commandments, and teaches others to do the same, shall be called least in the kingdom of heaven; but whoever keeps and teaches them, he shall be called great in the kingdom of heaven.* (Matthew 5:17-19)

As I read these verses, the realization began to sink into me that according to Jesus, God still rules His kingdom by Law. Jesus taught that God's Law must be fulfilled or perfected and not abolished or destroyed. He taught against annulling the Law, which means rendering it useless or without authority. Jesus also taught His followers to embrace God's lawful and righteous character rather than focusing on the Law as an end in itself. He warned against interpretations of God's Law that only served to circumvent its purpose of establishing God's reign.

From reading Jesus' Sermon on the Mount, it was clear to me that His teaching on the Law was meant to establish principles of interpretation of the Torah rather than to simply add new commandments. Jesus' teaching in Matthew chapter five is not an exhaustive commentary on every statute of the Law. I realized that His intention was ultimately to reveal God's purposes in giving the Law. Jesus' teaching revealed not a different law but rather a new and higher way to approach the Living God who is our reigning King. He taught and demonstrated to His disciples a way to live in greater holiness and obedience to God rather than the way of the legalistic Pharisees who had substituted the formality of God's laws for God Himself. Because the Pharisees were intent on literally keeping all 613 of the commands in the Torah, Jesus said to His followers, "For I say to you that unless your righteousness surpasses that of the scribes and Pharisees, you will not enter the kingdom of heaven" (Matthew 5:20).

However, I'm sure that Jesus' disciples had questions in their minds after the first portion of Jesus' teaching that day. Did they think He was reinforcing the laws concerning permitted foods, forever outlawing pork sausages and shrimp cocktails for His followers? What did Jesus mean by speaking about "fulfilling the law?" So, no doubt knowing that everyone would have questions, Jesus continues with six illustrations about what He means regarding Law in His kingdom. In most of them, Jesus quotes the written Law of Moses and then says "but I say unto you…" giving His own interpretation. In these six examples Jesus is clearly not adding six new commandments to the existing commandments in the Torah. In this, His most famous sermon, He is teaching His disciples New Testament principles for interpreting the whole Law. Perhaps one could say that He chose six illustrations, one illustration short of seven, the perfect number, to show his followers that the list was meant to be incomplete. It should be completed as His disciples lived out the principles or spirit of His teaching.

I knew that the Sermon on the Mount is our record of Jesus' most comprehensive teaching on the kingdom of God. It has been called the greatest moral teaching in history. I could not avoid the thought that these words are more than just Jesus' good recommendations for a happy life. They are foundational to our understanding of His kingdom. Jesus first illustration had to do with murder, something almost all societies view as unlawful and a criminal offense.

You have heard that the ancients were told, "You shall not commit murder" and "Whoever commits murder shall be liable to the court." But I say to you that everyone who is angry with his brother shall be guilty before the court; and whoever says to his brother, "You good-for-nothing," shall be guilty before the supreme court; and whoever says, "You fool," shall be guilty enough to go into the fiery hell. (Matthew 5:21-22)

Here, Jesus is quoting from the Ten Commandments. Often spoken of as universal moral laws for all humanity, these commandments are clearly part of God's Law for Israel, and the sixth commandment is against murder. The principle, or the spirit, of the Law according to Jesus is to quench the inner fire of anger and hatred before it becomes the act of murder. Jesus was teaching that the sin does not begin when we pick up a weapon in our hand to murder. The sin begins with anger that is harbored and nurtured in our own hearts. The law of Jesus' kingdom deals with sin at its root, at the source of transgression. God's ultimate purpose is reconciliation and unity, the healing of wounded and broken relationships and replacing anger with love.

In His second of six illustrations, Jesus said:

You have heard that it was said, "You shall not commit adultery"; but I say to you that everyone who looks at a woman with lust for her has already committed adultery with her in his heart. (Matthew 5:27-28)

The spirit of this law is purity of heart. God's purpose is to cleanse His people from sexual sin starting deep within the heart. Jesus had previously taught in the same sermon that the pure in heart are blessed with the ability to see God. Anyone who has ever wrestled with the sin of pornography or sexual addiction will testify that it takes an outpouring of God's grace to be free. In the Bible, Job said, "I have made a covenant with my eyes; How then could I gaze at a virgin?" (Job 31:1) Jesus said that this kind of purity in the inner man of the heart is the law of His kingdom.

Jesus' Sermon on the Mount continues with His laws concerning marriage, divorce and the keeping of promises. I learned that God hates divorce and that His covenant with Israel was compared in the Scriptures to marriage. One of the primary values in God's kingdom is faithfulness. God knows that in marriage a bedrock mutual commitment to work out hurts and differences is essential. The fact is that in most cases, when a husband and wife decide together to deal with the issues that are destructive to their marriage, reconciliation will result. Jesus forbade divorce except when there was sexual unfaithfulness, and He said that remarriage for anyone wrongly divorced is sin (Matthew 5:32). When Rita and I were married, we believed that God would always be the "third partner" in our union and that if we turned to Him, He would provide whatever we lacked in keeping us together for life.

Jesus also taught that God is a God of truth and that He

hates lying, but the devil is a liar by nature and the "father of lies" (John 8:44). The principle in Jesus' Sermon on the Mount is that in God's kingdom, the standard is honesty. In some nations today, before testifying in a court of law, you are required to publicly swear an oath of honesty, sometimes with your hand on a Bible. After swearing that oath to tell the truth, if you then lie, it is considered a crime called perjury and it is punishable by imprisonment. In the days of Jesus, people swore by a number of things considered sacred and Jesus condemned the practice. He said, "But I say to you, make no oath at all… let your statement be, 'Yes, yes' or 'No, no'; anything beyond these is of evil" (Matthew 5:34 and 37). Jesus taught that in His kingdom it is not necessary to swear at all; honesty should be the norm.

As I read the teaching of Jesus, I discovered how deeply His sayings had become embedded in the language and culture of England and then the United States. Phrases like "turn the other cheek" and "the meek will inherit the earth" and "salt of the earth" and "light of the world" were already familiar to me. However, I had never seen them in their proper biblical context until I read what Jesus taught:

> *You have heard that it was said, 'An eye for an eye, and a tooth for a tooth.' But I say to you, do not resist an evil person; but whoever slaps you on your right cheek, turn the other to him also.* (Matthew 5:38-39)

79

Jesus is opening the door to understanding one of the central pillars of God's reign in His heavenly kingdom. This is the nature and value of God's mercy and mankind's universal need for it. The relationship between justice and mercy is what Jesus described as being among the "weightier provisions of the law" (Matthew 23:23). The question is do we want justice or mercy? Are we seeking the satisfaction of revenge or the peace of reconciliation? If we want mercy for ourselves and those we love, how can we receive it without giving to others as well? Jesus is also teaching that your strength of endurance is almost always stronger than your enemy's power to afflict you. Any boxer who gets into a ring expecting to be hit only once will never become a champion. The trophy goes to the one who is still standing when the final bell rings. The strength to turn the other cheek is the strength we all need to be victors in life.

You have heard that it was said, "You shall love your neighbor and hate your enemy." But I say to you, love your enemies and pray for those who persecute you. (Matthew 5:43-44)

Jesus' law to love your enemy must be among the greatest truths of His kingdom. The principle is that it is preferable and more powerful to win the heart and mind of your enemy than to defeat him in war. Which of the two in the end will bring real and lasting peace? When there is human conflict and war, the resulting wounds are deeper than merely in the flesh. Even after violence subsides the survivors on both sides bear inner pain and dysfunction that continues to destroy lives. Justice must be diligently sought after and rigorously applied to the guilty. Still, in a multitude of cases, complete justice will never be achieved. The only solution in places like Northern Ireland, South Africa, and Rwanda has been to seek peace and reconciliation through the recognition of shared grief and pain. Hatred and genocide become possible when we de-humanize members of another group. Love begins with the recognition of our shared humanity. Only love can break the evil cycle of revenge and retribution.

After His six illustrations, Jesus summed up this part of His greatest sermon with the words, "Therefore you are to be perfect, as your heavenly Father is perfect" (Matthew 5:48). This statement connects to the words He used to begin His discourse on the laws of God. He started out by telling His disciples that unless their righteousness surpassed that of merely religious people, they would never enter His kingdom. There is a big difference between simply being "better" and being "perfect." Jesus was telling me to keep my mind fixed on things above because God's standards and, therefore, my own goals were not to be defined by this world. How could I make this heavenly truth a part of my life?

Since I was young, I have always enjoyed watching world-class athletes compete in track and field. They train so hard and make feats impossible to most other humans look easy! One of my favorite sports to watch is high jumping. They start at the incredible height of close to two meters and jump backwards! The way it works is when everyone has had a chance to jump at a certain level, the bar is raised and all the successful ones try again. This process is repeated until finally there is only one jumper who is successful and that person is declared the winner. Then, in some cases they raise the bar again to see if there is a new world or Olympic record. As a result, the bar is ultimately raised until no one is successful.

Reading in the Bible about God's laws, I felt it was a lot like high jumping. Let's say that God's requirement in the Torah is represented by placing the bar at a certain level. In the Ten Commandments, God says, "You shall not commit murder." Now, we all have to try to jump that bar. Those who fail are punished. Although some do fail, most of us have learned to jump at least that high.

Is Jesus saying that since He has fulfilled the laws of God there is to be no more "jumping" in God's kingdom? Is He saying that now we have unlimited grace, mercy and love in the New Testament so that we can remove the "bar" of God's lawful requirements? No, Jesus obviously did not say that. In fact, what He did teach in His Sermon on the Mount is that rather than removing the bar, He raised it! I could understand that people who were able to meet Jesus' perfect standards would not only please God, but they would also bring the culture of

His kingdom wherever they went. However, faced with these requirements, I knew I was not only guilty before God's laws, but I was destined to fail. Even if I loved Jesus and wanted to serve Him with all my heart, I simply could not "jump" high enough to win the prize of righteousness and my King's approval. If I had to successfully obey these perfect laws to enter Jesus' kingdom, what would become of me in the end? Who would save me from my failure?

CHAPTER 6

CHAPTER 6

The tall white concrete walls of Christ for the Nations Institute (CFNI) rose like an almost surreal watchtower from the suburban South Dallas landscape. I had hitchhiked down from Santa Fe to attend a summer session at the Bible school taught by a well-known Bible teacher named Derek Prince. Friends in Santa Fe had told us about a place in Dallas where young people could go as students to be taught by experienced leaders. I longed for that kind of teaching and arrived in a kind of dazed state, not knowing what to expect. Inside, the meeting hall was packed with hundreds of people and Brother Derek, as he was called, was speaking with passion about something called "deliverance." It had to do with identifying the demonic forces active in your life and asking Jesus to cast them out.

By now, I was getting accustomed to listening to Christian speakers and aware that many of them were much better communicators than the politicians, bureaucrats, and university lecturers that I had been previously exposed to. Clearly an Englishman, Derek Prince spoke with unusual conviction and authority. I had never heard anything like it. Soon I realized that I was among those who needed deliverance. Some young people from the staff began to pray for me and then brought me into a carpeted room at the side of the speaker's podium. It was already full of people praying out loud and there was a sense of urgency and authority as well as love and acceptance in the room. The staff members were putting their hands on my head and praying in bold voices. They were rebuking spirits of darkness and bondage. Soon, a deep sense of peace came over me, and I was able to leave that small prayer room.

After that experience, I knew that Rita and I were supposed to attend the Bible school in Dallas. We said goodbye to our friends in Santa Fe and drove an old 1956 Volkswagen "Beetle" as far as Wichita Falls, Texas where it died by the side of the road at night. We ended up giving it to a family who stopped to help us. They turned out to be Christians and later wrote us to say they got the car running again and named it Timothy after the apostle Paul's disciple in the New Testament. We continued in a rented car that took the last of the cash we had. Our friends in Santa Fe had given us a going away gift of $250 in the form of a money order; however, soon after we arrived at the school, Rita accidentally ran the money order through a washing machine, and it was destroyed. Our two years at CFNI were not off to a good start.

The classes at the school were stimulating and entirely focused on the Bible. Many of the incoming students were coming directly from high school and believing families. Others were already in their twenties, and some like us were coming out of counterculture lifestyles from various parts of the United States. I devoured the Bible-related studies and read chapters of the Bible every day. Each morning there was a chapel service which all the students were required to attend. Music and singing songs of worship and praise to God were an important part of the school and the memories of those inspiring times will be with me forever. Every week, during the school term, there was a different guest speaker with experience in some area of ministry. Pastors, evangelists, missionaries and Bible teachers shared their teaching and sometimes their life stories with the student body. I knew that I was growing in faith, but it was a surprisingly difficult path.

The main problem was me. I felt like I was on a spiritual and emotional rollercoaster. Some of the time I felt strong and capable of meeting God's demand for perfection. The rest of the time I knew I was failing. Although I was free of demonic control, my thoughts, will, and emotions were still not yielded completely to God. No matter how hard I tried, I could never remain for long in a place where I knew I was pleasing to Him. For the first time in my life the difference between right and wrong had real meaning to me. I had found the absolute truth I longed for in my university days. God and the Bible held the moral absolutes I was now convinced would have saved my friend John's life. The problem was that I couldn't live in that morality for more than a few hours and each time I failed, I felt even worse.

Impure thoughts and ungodly cravings seemed to inhabit my very being like maggots crawling through a rotting corpse. They were everywhere. In addition to problems with my thoughts, I was realizing that the deeper, underlying motives of my heart were suspect at best, and selfishly corrupt much of the time. I tried fasting to gain control over my inner life but soon found that even if I forced myself to stop eating, later I would sneak into the snack area and gorge myself on junk food and donuts. Feeling condemned and frustrated I began bursting out in uncontrollable anger, even lashing out cruelly at Rita when we were alone. Things were going from bad to worse, and I wondered how long I would be able to handle this before giving up and leaving. I knew that leaving the school would mean leaving Rita, and that leaving my wife would probably mean I would be leaving God too. I was trapped, and I was sinking.

At this very low point, two things helped me to survive spiritually and to persevere. One was having believing friends and mentors, and the other was finding useful work to do. Dennis Lindsay was the son of Christ for the Nation's founder, Gordon Lindsay. Gordon Lindsay was a well-known, traveling evangelist who had been at the forefront of the movement to restore spiritual gifts of healing to the Church. He had founded CFNI in 1970 and died the year before we arrived. Growing up as a preacher's son in Dallas, part of the "Bible Belt" of Middle America, Dennis came from about as different a world from me as anyone possibly could. In spite of our different backgrounds, he and his wife Ginger reached out to Rita and me. They invited us to dinner at their apartment on campus. We met their friends and family. Their lives of faith, though not easy, seemed natural and unforced. They had fun and enjoyed doing simple, non-spiritual things in addition to their ministry work. Just being with them was an encouragement and a much needed "reality check." I couldn't understand how in my rough, unpolished state someone like Dennis could see anything valuable in me. One day, he told me that he had learned not to try to choose his own friends. He said he let God choose his friends for him. I didn't fully realize it then but through friendship, Dennis was passing on to me valuable truths about the culture of God's kingdom.

As part of a class on evangelism that Dennis taught we took a field trip one night to hear Josh McDowell speak in Dallas. Josh was already well-known because of his book on apologetics *Evidence That Demands a Verdict*, which had come out just a few years earlier. He was ministering at First Baptist Church, then one of the largest churches in America led by legendary pastor Dr. W. A. Criswell. When Josh spoke, I was mesmerized by his command of the material and ability to communicate clearly. The spiritual and intellectual challenge of that evening left an enduring impression on me.

Another friend, a fellow student also named Dennis, helped me in quite another way. Since we had so little money, I was always looking for some kind of work. At first I tried to sell Amway products from door to door. There were blocks of apartment buildings in the neighborhoods around the campus, many of them filled with "welfare moms." That is, single mothers with small children living on low incomes. As I walked these streets, small armies of African-American kids would follow me crying out, "Hey man, you Bruce Lee? You Kung Fu?" If I did make it into one of the apartments to demonstrate the various home care products, I would soon end up giving the stock away because of the heartbreaking stories I usually heard from the single mothers.

I failed as an Amway salesman, but my student friend, Dennis came to our door one day and said, "God told me to give you my job." He was a commercial teller at the Guarantee Bank across the street from the school. I interviewed for the job and was hired on the strength of Dennis' recommendation. I went to my classes in the morning and worked every afternoon. Soon I was handling thousands of dollars in cash and checks each day, and in the evenings we had to account for every penny or else we couldn't go home. It was good training because after becoming a hippie in New Mexico, I hadn't even used numbers or been required to write legibly. The work raised my self-esteem and was an effective balance to the spiritual discipline of Bible school.

John Garlock was Dean of the Bible school and when he learned I had taught beginning Japanese language classes in an experimental project at Tufts University, he gave me an opportunity to teach Japanese to anyone interested at CFNI. A handful of students showed up, but one of them, a nineteen year old student named Bill Wood, who had never been outside of the United States, showed unusual zeal. Later, he moved to Japan, married a Japanese woman, and today he is a respected teacher in the area of false religions and cults. He is a gifted interpreter and has written a number of useful books in the Japanese language. In some of these early classes I began to experience a special kind of joy from the Lord when I would stand to teach. It was the beginning of a spiritual gift of teaching that would continue to emerge in the years that followed.

While I was struggling to meet the challenges of living a life guided by God's Spirit, Rita was grappling with understanding her own calling. From the time she first heard about Jesus in Santa Fe, she never denied her identity as a Jewish person. To her, Jesus was her Jewish Messiah, the sacrificial "Lamb of God" who had been sent by God to make atonement for her sin according to the requirements of God's Law, the Torah, given to her people in the Bible. In Dallas, we began to meet more Jews who shared a faith similar to Rita's. They came from all over the country, and each had his or her own story of coming to believe that their Jewish Messiah was Jesus, who they called

"Yeshua," His Hebrew name meaning "salvation." As Jews, they already had a covenant with God, and now they were finding fulfillment in the new covenant established through Jesus' sacrifice. They called themselves "Messianic Jews." This was to emphasize the point that while believing in Jesus and the New Testament, these Jews had not forsaken Jewish identity to become non-Jews, nor did they identify themselves as Gentile Christians. We soon learned that the term "Christian" is not used in the New Testament until the gospel message was taken by believing Jews to unbelieving Gentiles at the city of Antioch in what is today southern Turkey. This is recorded in the eleventh chapter of Acts, nine chapters after salvation and the Holy Spirit were first poured out upon the Jews of Jerusalem. I learned that since all His original disciples were Jews, faith in Jesus according to the Bible has its roots in Jewish identity. Nevertheless, it was clear to us there is a huge spiritual and cultural gap today between Jews who believe in Jesus, and those who do not.

Rita's father, Mel, had been deeply hurt and angered by her decisions to follow Jesus as her Jewish Messiah and then to marry me. A few months after our wedding, he visited a well-known rabbi in New York to ask for advice. It was not unheard of for Jewish parents to declare a child "dead" and cut off from the family for betraying their Jewish faith. According to what we later heard, this rabbi's daughter had recently been killed in an accident, and so he said to Mel, "Your daughter is alive.

94

You should do what you can to reconcile with her." As a result of that conversation, Mel wrote Rita and invited us to come to New York for Yom Kippur, the Jewish Day of Atonement to fast and pray with him. We agreed and that visit began to heal our relationship. Later, he asked us to renew our wedding vows in a ceremony in New York when both sets of our parents were able to attend and participate. This took place one year to the day from our original ceremony in Santa Fe and was the fulfillment of the vision I had received of a wedding ceremony that would include all our parents, reading from the Scriptures. God has His perfect timing.

Our two years at Christ for the Nations were spiritually formative ones that began the difficult process of restoring my character to the good plan that God had for me before I was born. Like a spiritual "boot camp" I was subjected not only to learning the Bible, but to moral discipline and difficult practical lessons in life, but by the end of our time there, I was beginning to feel that being a believer was a lifestyle I could somehow make my own. As graduation approached I was being urged by the leaders to launch out into ministry. We knew that God's plan for us was outside the United States and eventually Israel, but I didn't feel ready. There were still too many unanswered questions in my mind about the Bible and the specifics of my own calling. We didn't want to leave the flow of spiritual restoration that had begun in us and looked for a place where I could continue to study and grow. That was when we heard about a place called Melodyland in southern California. It was a large congregation located in Orange County with thousands in attendance and a School of Theology. I applied to the School of Theology and was accepted into the Masters of Divinity program.

CHAPTER 7

CHAPTER 7

During my days in Bible school I learned that God's grace is free, but it is not cheap. "Cheap grace" is a message that lowers the standards of God's laws or casts scorn on the value of divine law as the way God governs His eternal kingdom. I heard preachers on television say that the Old Testament is concerned with law, but the New Testament is about grace, and we have to choose between the two. In forcing us toward this false choice, they said that law means legalism, judgment, and condemnation, but grace is all about love and mercy. Their message was that Jesus paid the entire price for all of our sins once and for all; therefore, we are forever freed from the requirements of God's law by the free gift of grace.

What's wrong with that? Didn't Jesus die to give us His salvation as a free gift? Doesn't the New Testament teach that we are justified (made righteous before God) by faith in Him? Yes, this is true, but if I had stopped listening there, I might have come to the wrong conclusion about God's reason for saving me by grace. It was God's moral requirements in His laws that defined sin and convicted me as a sinner. Before I knew God's laws, I didn't have a need for grace at all. If God has high standards, then I need great grace to be declared by Him as righteous. But, if God has low standards, His grace does not need to be that amazing or precious. Any message that overtly or subtly by suggestion reduces the requirements of God's laws cheapens grace. One fact about human nature is that we all love finding bargains. Like the crowds swarming to a half-price sale in a shopping mall, a pastor or teacher who cheapens grace will find that at least initially a lot of people will be interested in attending his church. However, they may not be ready to go on to become disciples of Jesus.

I understood that the Bible teaches that "mercy triumphs over judgment" (James 2:13). Yes, that is true, but I also knew that mercy can never *replace* judgment. Mercy only has real value to me when I know I deserve judgment. I received mercy as a free gift of God's grace and began to appreciate it all the more because the Bible teaches that God always has and always will rule His kingdom by law. Mercy has to be the *exception* to the law. What if there was a judge in a city who always decided in every case to show mercy? Soon, every serial killer, rapist, child molester, and professional gangster would be lining up outside that judge's courtroom. No one would be punished. No one would be compelled to change, and all would go free. Is that God's kind of mercy or simply injustice?

Dietrich Bonhoeffer was a Christian pastor in Germany during the 1930s when Nazism was rising to power. I read in his book, *The Cost of Discipleship*, that God's mercy is not meant to be applied to everyone as a doctrine, but as a gift given personally and individually by God Himself to those who put their trust in His Son, Jesus. When God gives mercy, He does not nullify or change His own laws; thus, the one who receives mercy must afterwards seek to remain "hidden in Christ," which means to live in a way that meets the demands of God's righteousness. This process is called sanctification and results in discipleship. Bonhoeffer pointed out that justification by faith means that God justifies the sinner but not the sin. When I fell into sin and then turned to God through faith in Jesus, I received grace to be forgiven, and I was justified which means restored to righteousness. God said, "You are okay now. Go and sin no more." He wasn't saying to me, "Your sins are okay now. Don't worry about it anymore."

I saw that the laws of God's kingdom define His reign as sovereign ruler. These laws give believers moral authority and spiritual guidance to be personally changed and then to begin restoring God's purity and love to the cultures of this world. When God's kingdom is preached, sins embedded deep in culture like racial prejudice, political corruption, addictions, and other social dysfunctions will yield to the power of His lawful reign. People are not only saved but also transformed by the gospel of the kingdom. When Bonhoeffer served as a pastor in Germany, that nation was called the "cradle of the Reformation" and thought to be among the most "Christian" countries in Europe. However, the preaching of cheap grace had *Christianized* Germany but not transformed it. The majority of Lutheran Germans believed they were saved but lacked the moral authority and personal integrity to resist Nazism. The devastation that resulted was one of the hidden costs of cheap grace.

Martin Niemöller, also a Protestant pastor in Nazi Germany, spent seven years in concentration camps for opposing Hitler's control of the churches. After the war, he spoke out about his failure as a German Christian to stand against what he knew was evil. Here is one version of a famous poem attributed to him:

When the Nazis came for the communists,
I remained silent;
I was not a communist.

When they locked up the social democrats,
I remained silent;
I was not a social democrat.

When they came for the trade unionists,
I did not speak out;
I was not a trade unionist.

When they came for the Jews,

I remained silent;
I wasn't a Jew.

When they came for me,
there was no one left to speak out.

All humans are deeply flawed, and this is why we so desperately need God's grace. I learned that when Jesus died on the cross for my sins, the requirement of God's laws did not change. What did change was that for the first time God's requirements were satisfied—not by me, but by the atoning sacrifice of His own Son. Jesus was the only human to ever fully keep the laws of God. In doing so He opened the way for me to be, by faith in Him and by *abiding in Him*, declared righteous by God. Slowly and painfully I was beginning to appreciate the meaning and truly amazing quality of New Testament grace. God loves me. He wants me to be a moral and spiritual champion and believes that is what I am meant to be. The gospel message says that when I realize God's standards are not optional, it means an agonizing death to my efforts to please Him. The good news is that if I put my trust in Jesus and "die" in pursuit of His goals, the same Spirit that raised Jesus from His grave will begin to live in me! (Romans 8:11) The power of faith then rises in my heart from the ashes of my human inability. It's no longer me who is alive but God's Spirit who is alive inside of me. I start to believe I can do anything

He requires through His power working in my new life. I say with the apostle Paul, "I can do all things through Christ who strengthens me!" (Philippians 4:13) God is not only the judge of my life's efforts, He is also my coach and loving Father! He is committed to my success so that if I don't give up, I will begin meeting His highest standards. God's grace is more than His mercy which forgives my sin and failure. His grace is also the enabling power of the Holy Spirit in me to overcome the challenges of life in a broken world.

When the disciples asked Jesus about restoring the kingdom to Israel in Acts 1:6, He told them about the power of the Holy Spirit to be "witnesses." I learned that the word "witness" is related to the word for "martyr," someone who gives up his life for God. It was at this very point I found my greatest need for the power of God's grace. I discovered that developing a believing lifestyle was a process of first coming under the seemingly impossible standards of Jesus and then discovering His truly amazing grace to begin meeting those perfect requirements one by one. It was then, and continues to be, a lifestyle that consists of first dying to my personal, selfish desires and then rising again in new hope. I think this must be what Jesus referred to when He said "If anyone wishes to come after Me, he must deny himself, and take up his cross daily and follow Me" (Matthew 16:24). I found the struggle to be long and difficult but, in the end, a path toward freedom and life.

The New Testament teaches that the law of the Messiah

is a perfect law, a law of the Spirit and a law of liberty (James 1:25). I had previously thought, as did most of my generation, that law meant restrictions and punishment, not freedom, and I struggled with understanding God's laws as being laws of liberty. It made me consider what it means to be truly free, and I began coming to a new definition of freedom in my own life. Earlier in my life, I would have defined freedom as independence. Freedom meant being unconstrained by outside restrictions. As an American I had been taught to regard July 4th Independence Day as the symbol of American freedom. Now I began to realize that independence from England alone had not made Americans free; rather it was the drafting of the Constitution and the creation of new laws that guaranteed American freedoms.

What if I developed persistent pressure and pain in my chest and was taken to a hospital emergency room? Would I accept a physical examination conducted by one of the cafeteria cooks instead of a trained cardiologist? Of course not! What's the difference? The cardiologist has been required by law to study years in order to learn thousands of other laws that govern the functioning of a human body and especially the heart. That doctor has a powerful freedom to determine what is wrong with me and prescribe appropriate treatment. My freedom to live a healthy life is helped by medical professionals who take the time and effort to learn the laws of medicine. I gradually realized that everything is governed by law, whether it is mathematics and science, music, sports, or business. Since the days of the Magna Carta, the rule of law has proven to be the single most important political factor in the relative success and prosperity of nations. I once read a book titled *12 Books That Changed The World*. According to the author, one of those great books is *The Rule Book of Association Football*, which contains the rules of the game Americans call soccer. This game is played and watched by more people in the world than any other sport in history, and it is all based on a handful of simple rules. This made me realize that if you change the rules, you change the entire game. The "laws" of football bring intense enjoyment to millions every year. My conclusion is that there is no freedom without law. Bad laws restrict freedom; good laws mean more freedom. Does that mean perfect laws bring perfect freedom?

CHAPTER 8

CHAPTER 8

I was once told the story of a man who equated freedom with independence and wanted to find it. He was desperately poor and sought freedom from poverty, so he worked hard and eventually became wealthy. However, after becoming rich he found that he couldn't buy freedom from loneliness, and so he found a woman he cared for and decided to be married. Soon they had children, but the man felt trapped by his marriage relationship and the responsibility of raising a family. So he abandoned them, and then saw a newspaper advertisement for something called "space tourism." He could pay to be trained and sent beyond earthly restrictions into outer space! He enrolled in the program and once in space, he found himself confined by the tiny size of his spacecraft, so he embarked on a space walk in just a spacesuit. Yet he was still tethered to the spacecraft by an annoying and short "umbilical cord" of tubes and cables. Seeking the freedom of complete independence, the man uncoupled his connecting cord and drifted off into space. Now, at last, he was totally independent and, of course, totally dead.

Perhaps a better definition of freedom begins with having all your needs met while, at the same time, being protected from harm. If that is so, then my freedom began before I was born. When I was in my mother's womb, I didn't do anything wrong. All my needs were met, and I was completely protected and cared for. In Hebrew, the word for womb is *rechem*, which is closely related to the word *rachamim*, meaning "mercy." It is a big challenge for everyone to leave the protection and contented freedom of the womb and start to deal with the harshness and injustices of life in this world. Maybe this is why every healthy baby cries as soon as it is born!

If the baby in its mother's womb is better off than a dead space tourist, then freedom is not simply independence, but rather it is to be found through dependence and trust. We can't stay our whole lives in our mother's womb, but even after being born, we need a loving, protective environment to develop our full potential. The Bible actually says a lot about freedom. It has a very high value in God's kingdom. The Messianic prophecy that Jesus read in His own synagogue is found in Isaiah chapter sixty-one. Jesus read, "The Spirit of the Lord God is upon me, because the Lord has anointed me to bring good news to the afflicted; He has sent me to bind up the brokenhearted, to proclaim liberty to captives and freedom to prisoners."

Freedom is one of God's basic characteristics, and the Bible says all humans were created in the image of God. We are supposed to be like Him, and whether we believe in God or not, all of us have an inner longing for freedom. According to the Bible, God is free, but our sin shattered His image in us. We became slaves to sin. However when Jesus came, He told His followers in John chapter eight, "You will know the truth, and the truth will make you free. Everyone who commits sin is the slave of sin. The slave does not remain in the house forever; the son does remain forever. So if the Son makes you free, you will be free indeed." Of course, Jesus was teaching about moral freedom, that is, freedom of the heart. God's will is a heart set free from guilt, condemnation, regret, addiction and self-destruction. I learned that God wants me to be free, to be exactly who He created me to be. I also learned a deep truth about God and His kingdom: freedom in God's kingdom is defined and protected by law. I began to see that the Bible describes moral freedom as something that cannot be achieved or even understood apart from God's lawful reign.

I learned that Jesus' teaching raised the requirements of God's law to a perfect level and shifted the focus of obedience from outward behavior to inner integrity and commitment of the heart. Jesus taught that God's law was God ruling the inner man by a law of the heart or of the spirit. Clearly His teaching was radical but should not have been totally new to Israel. Centuries before Jesus, the prophet Jeremiah had written:

Behold, days are coming," declares the LORD, "when I will make a new covenant with the house of Israel and with the house of Judah, not like the covenant which I made with their fathers in the day I took them by the hand to bring them out of the land of Egypt, My covenant which they broke, although I was a husband to them," declares the LORD. "But this is the covenant which I will make with the house of Israel after those days," declares the LORD, "I will put My law within them and on their heart I will write it; and I will be their God, and they shall be My people. They will not teach again, each man his neighbor and each man his brother, saying, 'Know the LORD,' for they will all know Me, from the least of them to the greatest of them," declares the LORD, "for I will forgive their iniquity, and their sin I will remember no more." (Jeremiah 31:31-34)

Interestingly, the words in the Hebrew text for "new covenant," *brit hadasha*, are the same words used in the modern Hebrew language for the New Testament. Most Jews today regard the New Testament as a book that is foreign to them and not Jewish. Many are surprised to read in the Jewish Bible that Jeremiah prophesied God would make a "new testament" with none other than the people of Israel and Judah. He said that it was God's intention to write His Law in the hearts of His people, and this would mean that each individual would have a personal knowledge of and relationship with the Living God. Jeremiah's prophecy is a description of God's Spirit reigning inside each person. Centuries later, in the New Testament, the apostle Paul described the difference between being ruled by rules, that is, by the "letter" of God's Law, and being ruled by His Spirit. Paul wrote, "… our adequacy is from God, who also made us adequate as servants of a new covenant, not of the letter but of the Spirit; for the letter kills, but the Spirit gives life" (2 Corinthians 3:5-6).

Here is a story that illustrates the difference between the letter and the spirit of the Law and also the process of coming to spiritual maturity. Think of yourself as a three-year-old. Outside your house is a busy street that curves, and at that curve is a crosswalk and a traffic light. Your father takes you by the hand out to the sidewalk and tells you under no circumstances are you allowed to step out on the street when the light at the crosswalk is red. There are no exceptions whatsoever. If you disobey, you will be punished. It is your loving father's law.

Ten years later, you are thirteen and feeling very grown up. You no longer need your father to take you across the street. You go by yourself now, and no one needs to tell you not to step out on that busy street when the light is red. You have internalized your father's teaching by now and over the years you have seen some very bad accidents at that same street corner. What was once his law is now your own. Your obedience is habitual and automatic at an almost unconscious level. This is what Jeremiah referred to when he wrote about God's Law being written on the hearts of His people.

Then one day while you are standing obediently at the curb waiting for the red light to change, something happens that tests your obedience to your father's law and your understanding of his character at the same time. You see an elderly lady walking unsteadily with a cane entering the crosswalk from across the street. She is either partially blind or disoriented, and she evidently has not noticed that the light is still red. She is walking into danger. Instantly, you know two things: First, in a moment a car will come sweeping around that curve, and it will not have time to stop before hitting her. Second, if you immediately run out in the street, you could probably help her back to the curb in time. But what should you do? The light is still red. Your father has always strictly forbidden you from stepping into the street until the light changes, and now that law is written on your own heart.

On the other hand, even at thirteen, you are mature enough to realize that your father's intention in giving you his law about the red light was to protect your life and the lives of others. You know His character and that saving a human life is one of his highest values. So you immediately leap from the curb, run to the lady and help her back to safety! This is an illustration of the law of the Spirit of life in Christ Jesus that Paul wrote about in Romans chapter eight. If you had stuck with the "letter" of the law, the lady could have been badly injured or killed. You broke the letter of the law in order to fulfill the higher requirement in the spirit of the law. You did this in confidence that after saving the lady, your father, having seen all from his window and emerging from the house, would not scold you for transgressing his rule, but rather embrace you and congratulate you for a job well done. He might even say, "Son, now you are mature and ready to start making important decisions for yourself."

There are numerous biblical examples of Jesus' obedience to the spirit rather than the letter of the law, but one that immediately comes to mind is found in John chapter five. Here Jesus encounters a crippled man at the pools of Bethesda in Jerusalem. The man had been lying by the pools for thirty-eight years until the day Jesus healed him and told him to take up his old pallet and walk! The religious people from Jerusalem, who must certainly have known him, saw the man carrying his pallet, but they did not immediately rejoice with him in his miraculous healing; rather they criticized him for carrying a load on the Sabbath – a violation of the Torah.

The apostle Paul certainly knew the Torah better than most people in his day. As a young man he was a disciple of Gamaliel, one of the leading rabbis of his generation. Paul was being groomed for the *Sanhedrin*, the top religious ruling council in the land. In one of his letters, he wrote he was a "Pharisee of the Pharisees," that is, a religiously observant Jew who was zealous to observe all the 613 commands in the Torah. However, after He came to faith in Jesus, he ministered with a powerful liberty and inspired many to follow his example. I wondered, "How did he achieve such freedom from the restrictive aspects of his religion and culture to become so spiritually fruitful?".

As I read the New Testament, I realized that Paul devoted much of his teaching to our relationship with God's laws. He deeply appreciated the Torah as God's word but understood that the power of sin made pursuing obedience to the literal commands result in legalism, bondage and ultimately spiritual death (Romans 7:8-13). On the other hand, life outside the bounds of God's Law ends in lawlessness and separation from God's reign, a different but equally dangerous result. Paul applied himself to solving the problem of how believers can progress from the letter of the Law that kills us through legalistic condemnation to the spirit of the Law that sets us free without losing the lawful reign of God in the process.

Paul's conclusion is that God Himself provided the answer to that question by sending His own Son, Jesus, to come to us as a man, that is, someone under the laws of God. Jesus was the only human to fully obey God by living perfectly in the Spirit of God's Law. Yet, He was condemned and submitted to death on behalf of all of us who could not keep either the letter or the spirit of the Law. Paul said that by trusting in God and faithfully following Jesus' example, the Spirit that raised Him from the dead would be given to us. I was learning that my own human nature would always be opposed to God's reign, but if I identified myself with Jesus' death, then the eternal life active in His resurrection would also be mine! The Spirit of

God was giving me an ability to obey God that people should have only have after their fleshly nature has been destroyed. Paul's statement in Romans chapter eight, verse four summed it up as follows: "so that the requirement of the Law might be fulfilled in us, who do not walk according to the flesh but according to the Spirit."

I understood that since Jesus has died and risen from the grave, His Spirit can live in me and write the laws of God inside of me while also giving me the power to obey them. Here in the heart of the New Testament is the fulfillment of what Jeremiah prophesied so many years before when he said that God would write His Torah on the hearts of His people. God doesn't condemn me for stumbling while trying to please Him; rather He condemns the sin in me that is opposed to God's will for my life (Romans 8:1-3). Paul, who knew the Torah so well, wrote that by the power of God's Spirit in us, we can live in such a way that God's requirements are fulfilled. I was struggling toward a freedom that is not found through an escape from God's laws. On the contrary, in pursuit of *mastering* God's laws I was beginning to taste personal victory. The Holy Spirit does not lead us into a culture of lawlessness. Instead it is the *lawfulness* of the Spirit of life that comes from Jesus, the King Himself, that sets us free to know God personally and begin a new life in obedience to His decrees. I was learning that whenever I yielded to the Spirit of God's laws, I could also find freedom.

It occurred to me that living according to the Spirit of God's laws was somewhat like learning to drive a car. I had first received a driving license at the age of sixteen, and by the time I was in Bible school, I had been driving for years. Piloting a motor vehicle even at normal speeds is not a trivial task. Only a few seconds of bad driving can make almost anyone a mass killer! The fact is that when you drive, you are functioning within a highly complex matrix of laws. Laws of physics govern the way the car handles at different speeds, road conditions, and whether you are driving straight or turning a corner. Engineering laws were applied to the design and construction of the car and its engine and complex laws of chemistry to its fuel. While driving, we even have to be constantly aware of laws that govern human behavior. A child playing with a ball by the side of the road is likely to act differently than an elderly person or someone on a bicycle. Then, of course, there are the local traffic laws with signs, painted lines, and traffic lights to be aware of. Many laws converge on the driver of an automobile, and yet, after a few years of practice, we function safely within those laws, all the while listening to music or thinking about something else! Certainly, you have to be constantly alert to drive a car safely, but my point is that when you have mastered the skills needed to drive, most of it becomes nearly unconscious and habitual. This is an illustration of how we are meant to internalize the Spirit of God's laws. The unselfconscious lawfulness

118

demonstrated in Jesus' own life is the goal of all our spiritual learning and discipline.

CHAPTER 9

CHAPTER 9

After leaving Dallas, we came to California in 1976 not really knowing what to expect. We soon discovered it was a time of powerful spiritual change. The "Jesus Movement" had swept through a few years earlier, and thousands of hippies and counterculture youth had become Christians. Their influence had deeply impacted the church scene. In nearby Costa Mesa, Calvary Chapel, led by Pastor Chuck Smith, had grown explosively and spawned a new ministry called *Maranatha! Music*. Christian musicians like Larry Norman, Honeytree, Andre Crouch, and Chuck Girard along with groups like Love Song, Parable and 2nd Chapter of Acts were creating a contemporary sound for people like us just starting out into new lives of faith. Not long after, a young musician named Keith Green would burst upon the scene using a driving rock style to preach a message of repentance and radical commitment to the gospel. A few years after we arrived, a former professional musician turned minister named John Wimber would build the Vineyard movement in Orange County and move into a converted mega-store not far from where we lived.

Melodyland took its name from a former theatre-in-the-round located across the street from Disneyland in Anaheim. At one time it had featured the largest bar in Orange County, but Pastor Ralph Wilkerson had purchased the property and changed it into a vibrant Christian center. Pastor Wilkerson was known for having brought Kathryn Kuhlman's ministry of healing to California and his gift was evangelism. Often he would give an altar call in the midst of the music service without ever preaching a message and dozens of people would come forward to receive salvation and healing. Melodyland Christian Center had grown to close to ten thousand in attendance by the time we arrived. Attached to the congregation was the School of Theology called MST headed by Dr. J. Rodman Williams.

Classes at MST were both intellectually stimulating and spiritually refreshing. We studied biblical languages, church history, and New and Old Testament theology along with newer subjects like the use of charismatic gifts. Our instructors came from diverse backgrounds, but many of their personal histories were very similar. They had served in traditional Protestant denominations for most of their lives, but they were drawn by spiritual hunger and biblical conviction to the charismatic movement and the gifts of the Holy Spirit. When they openly admitted to speaking in tongues, fellow ministers who had been their colleagues for decades asked them to leave their denominations. In those days, in many traditional and some evangelical churches, if you raised your hands in worship, ushers would come and tell you to put them down! At MST, every class began with a time of worship and prayer. There were several hundred students, but soon we were forming a close community through networks of friendships and shared interests. J. Rodman Williams was affectionately known as "Dr. Rod" and he and his wife Jo became a spiritual dad and mom to many of the students. In our classes, we were challenged by the professors to question our beliefs as well as defend them. Leaders we met at MST as well as through the church inspired us to reach out and grow into ministry positions. The more senior students served as intern pastors at Melodyland, helping the pastoral staff with counseling, weddings, and other duties.

I still struggled, although less frequently, with bringing my inner life under the authority of the Holy Spirit. There were times when pressures built up to the point I felt overwhelmed and wondered how I could go on. Toward the end of my time at MST I also served as an intern pastor at the church. Every Sunday, we were at each service ready to counsel and pray with the dozens who came forward during the service. When an altar call was made, and people came forward, the interns would go with them into an adjacent prayer room. One of the staff pastors would give instructions, and then we would pair off with the people and begin by asking them why they had come forward. One Sunday, I was feeling unusually low and unable to counsel anyone. Nevertheless, I dutifully went with the group into the prayer room. As the pairing off process took place, I closed my eyes and silently prayed that no one would be left for me. As I opened my eyes, I noticed that only my friend Dave, another intern, was left. *Great!* I thought, *I'll just go over to him and confess my problem and he will pray for me!* When I went to Dave and told him what I was going through, I thought he would treat me with compassion as if I were just another person asking for prayer. Instead, he looked at me and laughed out loud. I was shocked, a little embarrassed, and didn't know what to say. Dave leaned over and whispered in my ear, "I'm sorry I laughed, but it's because I came in here for the very same reason!" After that we agreed to meet together a couple times a week in the early morning for worship, prayer, and mutual encouragement. Over the years, spiritual friends like Dave were vitally important in my growth as a believer.

During this time in California, I also learned that God does not change His standards for anyone. As the Bible says, there is truly "no partiality" with God. However, the Lord does give us His grace as we go on with Him. Amazing grace is more than God's mercy and forgiveness when we turn to Him through our failure. It is also His power and encouragement that enables the willing heart to meet and overcome the challenges of temptation and disillusionment to live a moral life. It was heartbreaking when some of my friends broke their covenant relationships of marriage. One or two even appeared to walk away from the path of following Jesus. Someone once said the life of faith is a marathon and not a sprint. A few leaders I knew even fell from their positions of responsibility and dropped out of the race for a while. One day, I was invited to the home of an elderly woman living in southern California named Corrie Ten Boom. She was a Dutch Christian whose family had hidden Jews in Holland during the Second World War. They were eventually betrayed, imprisoned by the Nazis, and her father and sister perished in the concentration camps. Corrie survived and later wrote a book called *The Hiding Place* in which she described their lives, the decisions they made as a family, and the ordeal that resulted. Corrie and her family became for me a real life example of believers who stretched out to reach God's highest standards and finished their race victoriously.

Another incident comes to my mind about my time as an intern. As one of our duties we were required to serve as pastors-on-call for the all-night hotline operated by Melodyland. One evening it was my turn, and the telephone rang at about two in the morning. It was a hotline operator saying they needed a pastoral call at a certain address about a twenty-minute drive away. When I asked for details, he said there had been a report of domestic violence. When he said violence, I asked why he didn't call the police instead. The operator insisted that in his opinion, it was a pastoral call that was needed. I agreed to go, but Rita wisely cautioned me to ask another intern on call to accompany me.

When we arrived at the address given by the hotline, it was

nearly three in the morning. It was an apartment in one of the vast suburbs that cover Orange County. Inside, the place was a mess. Furniture was overturned, lamps were broken, and two young men were holding a third man, their roommate, on the floor. While they restrained him, he struggled and kept repeating, "They said they would leave me alone!" It turned out that he had been drinking earlier that evening, come home, and begun to act violently. The roommates didn't know who he thought was harassing him, but we knew immediately it was demonic. We began to pray over him, forcefully casting out the evil spirits. It took about forty-five minutes, but eventually we felt the Holy Spirit gain the upper hand and the young man grew quiet and stopped struggling. As he regained control of himself, he told us what had happened to him.

He said he had become involved in a group of Satan worshippers near San Diego, and sometime earlier had witnessed the killing of a homeless woman in one of their "ceremonies." Ever since that time he had been pursued by a terrifying presence that would not let him go. He had turned to drinking to escape, but it resulted in a violent reaction earlier that evening. We told him that he was free for the time being but would need to find complete spiritual protection through faith in Jesus. We knew we were out of our league when it came to counseling him or giving advice on any legal aspects of his experience, so we gave him the number of a staff pastor and left. His roommates, who were Mormons, said they had never seen anything like the power in Jesus' name we had just demonstrated in their living room. As we drove away, I reflected that it had just been a few years earlier when I had been in need of spiritual deliverance of a different kind.

A number of us in the MST Master's degree program were chosen for a spiritual leadership group meant to prepare us to help those in need of pastoral care. One of our professors, Dr. Doyle Book, who had been a missionary to Japan for many years, led the group. On one of our first retreats at a beautiful center in the California mountains, we sat around the fireplace after dinner. Doyle asked us all to share our personal stories of how we became believers in Jesus. When it came to my turn, I told the story of my friend John's suicide, its effect on me, and how I had turned to the Lord. I was still uncomfortable telling the part about his death and my involvement in it. Immediately, after I finished Doyle looked directly at me and in the presence of all the others said in a firm voice, "Peter, be healed in the name of Jesus!" The love and authority in his voice caused a powerful and deep change in me. From that moment on, I never again felt the despair and discomfort connected with that pivotal chapter in my life.

After moving to California, I knew right away we had left the "womb" of our Bible school community in Dallas to face the challenges of life in a much more open environment. This had a sobering effect and ultimately forced me to strive toward a new level of maturity as a disciple of Jesus. Here I was exposed to the idea and practice of ministry as a profession and even as a "business." Christian television was becoming widespread and sometimes the outright commercialization of the gospel over the airwaves was shocking. In those years, I also came in contact with people caught up in spiritual deception and false doctrine. The realization that although God's grace is offered to all, not everyone feels compelled to obey Him caused in me a greater desperation to follow the truth. I became more thankful for the grace of God in choosing someone with as many faults as me to be His servant and keeping me on the right track.

During our time in California, Rita and I also struggled financially. Using my earlier work experience in the bank in Dallas, I applied for and got a job in a local bank, but the salary was so low we could only barely pay our rent and tuition. Rita was also beginning to pursue her Master's degree in Intercultural Communication at nearby California State University at Fullerton. Then our car broke down on the freeway, and I had no money to pay for its repairs. We borrowed the money to fix the car, but I knew that I would have to find a better job.

A few months earlier, in one of my classes at MST I had met a fellow student named Don who had been an IBM executive before becoming a believer and seeking a future in ministry. He said that while excited about learning theology, he had a wife and two teen-aged children who needed his support. I prayed for him after class and a few weeks later he

130

told me that he'd found a job in a local computer company called General Automation. This was around 1978 at the height of the minicomputer "revolution." Before the days of personal computers, these small computers were leading the way in moving computing power out of air-conditioned rooms staffed by white-coated specialists onto factory floors and into warehouses and offices. Today, it's hard to imagine that these machines were considered small, powerful, and inexpensive. They were the size of small washing machines. 128 K of "core" was considered a lot of internal memory, and it could be expanded with additional boards holding 32 K, each costing about $20,000! People like Bill Gates and Steve Jobs were just starting out, and their names were still not known to the public. The minicomputer world was dominated by companies with names like Prime, Data General, Microdata and later, Digital Equipment Corp. known simply as DEC.

Being in debt started me searching for a better paying job and when he heard about it, Don offered to arrange an interview at the company where he was now in charge of sales in the western region. Later, Don told me he had received a vision of me that he thought was from God. While in prayer, he saw me sitting at a computer terminal with others from different countries crowding around me, and I was explaining something on the screen to them. I told him that had to be a vision from God because at the time I didn't know the first thing about computers!

Because of Don's insistence, I was interviewed and although I clearly did not have the necessary skills or background, General Automation offered me ten weeks of training. If I didn't prove I belonged in the company, they would fire me. The salary was roughly twice what I was earning at the bank, so I took the job. Right away, I started taking classes in computer logic, operating systems and computer languages. These subjects are familiar to many school children today, but then words like binary digits, megabytes, and disk memory represented a very new and challenging world. Surprisingly, from the start I loved it. The closest I had ever come to a computer during my university days was during a student strike on campus when activists sat down in the school's computer center to obstruct its operation. At General Automation, the logic of programming the machines and the whole process of manufacturing and marketing them was beautiful and fascinating to me. I learned to program Fortran and COBOL applications and was sent to work at a customer site, Coca Cola of Los Angeles. Their headquarters building in the downtown area was an historical landmark, shaped like a huge ocean liner. My first program, a billing application with almost two thousand lines of code, actually ran and at the end of six months, General Automation offered me a regular job.

Soon I was moving around the company in various positions from Programmer to Sales Analyst to the Education Department where I developed and taught software courses to our customers and new employees. They crowded around my computer terminal as I taught them. By my second year, Don's vision had come to pass! Sometime later, a friend of mine from our days at Tufts University who once made animated commercials for Boston television stations came out to California to make movies. Steve visited our offices, and I showed him the factory floor where automated machines were busy filling computer boards with chips and other components. Steve was intrigued and began talking about a story he was working on that involved someone accidentally entering the electronic world within a computer. Later, he wrote and directed the movie *TRON*. It eventually won an Oscar for technical achievement and is now considered the forerunner of today's computer animation movies. I still have a copy of the script he sent me in 1980.

My job at General Automation proved to be an integral part of God's plan for our lives. By the time I was ready to graduate from MST, I was already working in the marketing department helping to launch new software products. The company was beginning to send me to train others in countries like England, Japan, and the Philippines. Rita and I knew by this time that rather than going directly to Israel, we would first serve in Japan. Pastor Wilkerson invited us to join him at a national ministers' conference held in Ise, Japan. There he shared the platform with Dr. Yonggi Cho from Korea, and I was given a speaking opportunity as well. It was an encouraging and exciting experience for me.

Later that year we were ready to launch out to Japan, but at the time it was the most expensive country in the world. It would take us years of raising support from individuals and churches to pay for even one year of life in Tokyo. On the other hand, by then I had the beginnings of a resume and several years' experience in the new world of computers. I sent letters to several Japanese companies and was eventually hired by Nippon Electric Company, or NEC, one of the giants in the Japanese computer and telecommunications industry. They moved us to Tokyo and helped us find housing. I joined the army of dark suited "salarymen" on the Tokyo subways, and we also began looking for opportunities to serve others through our faith and growing understanding of God's kingdom.

CHAPTER 10

CHAPTER 10

While still in California, Rita earned her Master's degree in Intercultural Communication, and I had also been exposed both in seminary as well as in the computer industry to teaching people of many nations and races. As soon as we arrived in Japan, we began to experience firsthand the powerful and often invisible influence that culture exerts on everyone within its sphere. A wise man once said, "We don't know who discovered water, but we know it wasn't a fish!" Our own culture is like that in that it is usually too close, too much a part of us to be viewed objectively. It surrounds us, always touching our lives, and like the fish trying to inspect its watery environment, we find it transparent to our eyes.

The word culture comes from the word, to *cultivate*, that is, to grow, tend, foster or nurture. We use this word when we talk about "cultured pearls" or "culturing bacteria" in a laboratory. Our human cultures have a powerful role in our development as individuals and social beings. They provide an active environment for growth that molds the way we think, act, and speak. Culture's influence begins at the earliest stages of our lives and its most significant impact is found in areas "under the radar" of our awareness and the control of our conscious thoughts. Over the years, culture powerfully and quietly molds our subconscious. The way we "see" and evaluate the contribution of others, how we understand our surroundings, what we notice, and what we ignore are influenced and limited by it.

It is increasingly well-documented that social values embedded in culture are a key factor in determining the wealth or poverty of nations. Different cultures respond differently to war, famine, disease, financial deprivation, and other challenges. Some cultures thrive while others languish. Harvard Professor and author Samuel Huntington studied the comparative economic growth of Ghana and South Korea over a period of thirty years. In the 1960s their economies were very similar in size and type. By the 1990s, South Korea's economy was fifteen times larger than Ghana's. Huntington says:

Undoubtedly, many factors played a role, but it seemed to me that culture had to be a large part of the explanation. South Koreans valued thrift, investment, hard work, education, organization and discipline. Ghananians had different values. In short, cultures count.

In Huntington's seminal 1993 *Foreign Affairs* article titled,

"The Clash of Civilizations?" he wrote, "It is my hypothesis that the fundamental source of conflict in this new world will not be primarily ideological or primarily economic. The great divisions among humankind and the dominating source of conflict will be cultural."

Is cultural conflict inevitable? Anthropologist, Edward Hall, in his book *Beyond Culture* wrote,

> *...the future depends on man's being able to transcend the limits of individual cultures. To do so, however, he must first recognize and accept the multiple hidden dimensions of unconscious culture, because every culture has its own hidden, unique form of unconscious culture.*

The seemingly omnipresent power of "unconscious" culture has even found a place of respect in the management of today's corporations. In large, successful companies, one of top management's primary roles is to shape and/or guard positive corporate culture. Once an organization's culture is molded in a certain way, external rules to control behavior are less necessary. In their best-selling book on business management, *In Search of Excellence*, authors Thomas Peters and Robert Waterman, Jr. wrote:

Without exception, the dominance and coherence of [corporate] culture proved to be an essential quality of the excellent companies. Moreover, the stronger the culture and the more it was directed toward the marketplace, the less need was there for policy manuals, organization charts, or detailed procedures and rules.

The loss of good corporate culture can also be powerful in a negative way. In March, 2012, Greg Smith resigned from the Wall Street investment firm, Goldman Sachs. In his open letter to the *New York Times* he wrote:

It might sound surprising to a skeptical public, but culture was always a vital part of Goldman Sachs' success. It revolved around teamwork, integrity, a spirit of humility, and always doing right by our clients. The culture was the secret sauce that made this place great and allowed us to earn our clients' trust for 143 years. It wasn't just about making money; this alone will not sustain a firm for so long. It had something to do with pride and belief in the organization. I am sad to say that I look around today and see virtually no trace of the culture that made me love working for this firm for many years. I no longer have the pride, or the belief.

Some experts say that culture is much like an iceberg

floating in the sea. Because of its great weight, only a small portion of an iceberg is visible. The bulk of it is beneath the surface where, as in the case of the Titanic, it can pose an extreme danger to those who get too close without taking precautions. The surface elements of culture are obvious things like clothing, food preferences, tastes in music and art, language, and communication styles. The deeper and weightier aspects of culture are values and beliefs. What makes them less visible and harder to change is that much of this part of culture is unspoken and embedded in the unconscious. Often we are not aware of these deep-seated beliefs and values resident in different cultures, or even our own. We can only understand them indirectly through the behavior that springs from them. Because they can penetrate beyond the surface, sometimes, legends, heroes and children's stories reveal more about culture than experts can tell you.

As we struggled to meet the challenge of Japanese culture, I became even more aware of my identity as an "ambassador" of God's kingdom. We did not come to Japan in order to bring our version of Western culture with us, but rather our calling was to represent the culture of God's kingdom! While the word culture does not appear in the Bible, there are laws, traditions, festivals and many stories of heroes, kings, warriors and miracle workers in it. The powerful concept of culture is represented in the Bible by at least two other words. The "world" refers to godless, pagan culture and the "Law" refers to the divinely given culture of Israel. The apostle John wrote to His disciples, "Do not love the world, nor the things in the world" (1 John 2:15a). The New Testament Greek word for world is *kosmos*, from which we derive the English words "cosmetic" and "cosmopolitan." It means the interlocking system of things and appearances that characterize this present age. In the verse above, John, a Jewish disciple, may be using Hebrew parallelism to equate the world with the material benefits of the world. These "things" must never be the object of our devotion. Jesus told Nicodemus, a religiously observant Israeli leader, that "God so loved the world [kosmos] that He gave His only begotten Son that whoever believes in Him will have everlasting life" (John 3:16). Jesus showed that in spite of the world's rejection of Him, God still cares enough about His fallen creation to sacrifice what He loves most in order to redeem it.

From the example of Israel in the Bible as well as by examining the nations in which we live, it is not difficult to see the connection between culture and law. All cultures have laws both written and unwritten. The laws embedded in every culture serve to define and protect the values people in the culture hold dear. Even a casual reading of the first five books of the Bible (called the Torah, Law, Pentateuch or Books of Moses) show us that God's Law for Israel included commands concerning business, real estate transactions, family relationships, sexual morality, education, justice in the courts, foods to eat and not eat, clothes to wear and not wear, songs to sing, values to teach children, attitudes that are praiseworthy and those that are not, an entire annual calendar, basic health care, sanitation of public areas, and many other important topics. According to the Torah the entire nation of Israel was meant to be "holy," that is, reserved or set aside for God's own use. The priests were appointed for a special religious role, but there were no "second class citizens" in Israel according to God. All of society and culture was meant to reflect the sovereign Lord's glory and lawful reign. God's Law was meant to define Israel's lifestyle as well as enshrine and protect their most sacred beliefs. It is easy to see that the core of Israel's culture, and therefore the culture of God's kingdom, was His divine Law.

As I matured as a disciple and became more practiced at functioning in the lawful freedom of God's Spirit, I became increasingly aware that all the national cultures I was familiar with had good points and some dysfunctional aspects too. Around me I saw love, justice, and acceptance as well as cruelty, sexual exploitation, and racism. I also began to understand and inwardly sense God's great desire to heal all nations by imparting in them the lawful culture of His kingdom. Jesus sent His disciples into the world with these words, "Go and make disciples of all the nations" (Matthew 28:19). These realizations drew me increasingly to seek in the Bible for keys to my own personal role in this huge challenge.

The apostle Paul was an orthodox Jew, raised as a Roman

citizen outside of Israel in Tarsus (which is now southern Turkey), and then groomed to be a rabbi under Gamaliel, one of the leading Jewish religious leaders of his day. Because of his background, Paul was uniquely suited for the cross-cultural understanding that God gave him by revelation and the apostolic ministry that resulted. What was the result of Paul's radical identification with Jesus' death and resurrection? He first became an outcast and was considered an enemy to be hunted and killed by his own countrymen and former friends. He was let down in a basket from the wall of Damascus so that he could elude his enemies. He escaped, outside the city, but at the appointed time, re-entered his home culture, empowered by his new faith. Paul understood and taught others about the freedom he found in the culture of God's kingdom. Here's what he said about his newfound liberty:

> *For though I am free from all men, I have made myself a slave to all, that I might win the more. And to the Jews I became as a Jew, that I might win Jews; to those who are under the Law, as under the Law, though not being myself under the Law, that I might win those who are under the Law; to those who are without law, as without law, though not being without the law of God but under the law of Christ, that I might win those who are without law. To the weak I became weak, that I might win the weak; I have become all things to all men, that I may*

144

*by all means save some. And I do all things for the sake
of the gospel, that I may become a fellow partaker of it.*
(1 Corinthians 9:19-23)

No man except Jesus Himself brought the teaching of
God's kingdom to as many as Paul. His inspired letters still lead
people to God's kingdom almost 2,000 years after they were
written. Trained as a rabbi, he knew God's Law better than
most men of his day, yet through faith in Jesus, he experienced
freedom few have attained since his time. Paul's freedom gave
him the flexibility to represent the eternal kingdom of God and
still embrace the cultural identity of the people to whom He was
sent. Paul had the freedom and spiritual ability to become the
servant of many, both Jews and Gentiles, and the result was his
transforming apostolic ministry of cross-cultural evangelism.

Paul was first and foremost a follower of his Messiah Jesus
who challenged all His disciples to deny themselves and lay
down their own personal lives in order to serve others (Matthew
16:24). Paul's sacrifice, his "death" to his own religious identity
and his familiar culture, opened the door for him to fulfill
his unique calling. He was able to adapt to whatever culture
he was in. Did this show a lack of integrity? Should we call
Paul a "cultural chameleon?" No, he was obeying a higher,
unchanging truth, a divine law, being "obedient to the heavenly
vision" (Acts 26:19). He was demonstrating the culture of
God's kingdom. As I read about Paul's understanding and

achievements, I deeply desired to find the same freedom and to be one of those who followed in his footsteps.

CHAPTER 11

CHAPTER 11

Tokyo in the 1980s was remarkably different from the Tokyo I remembered from my boyhood twenty years earlier. In those days, Japan was struggling to catch up economically with the West. Now Japan had not only caught up but surpassed almost every other country in the world. By then, the Japanese economy had become about the size of all of Europe combined. Only the United States still maintained its lead, and some were predicting that soon it too would fall behind Japan. A well-known American scholar, Ezra Vogel, published a book in this period called, *Japan as Number One – Lessons for America*. The Japanese edition of Vogel's book became a huge bestseller and new books on Japanese business management seemed to be appearing almost weekly.

I went to work in the heart of Tokyo for one of the largest electronics and telecommunications companies in the world. Nippon Electric Corp., or NEC, had about 12,000 employees just in the area where I worked around Tamachi station. I was part of the marketing division as an employee on contract and assigned a desk in the Number Two Annex Building. There I began to be immersed in "salaryman" culture. I learned that the salaryman was an honored "soldier" in the Japanese business "army." We wore our dark suits with the small golden company pin on the lapel with pride and sat in large open offices without partitions between the desks. Most of the other employees in my department traveled up to two hours by train to reach the office in the morning, and we often stayed at work much later than I was accustomed to in the United States.

Japan has changed a lot since I worked for NEC, but it is still unique in the amount of self-sacrifice in the service of social order that is required by spoken and unspoken rules that are built into the culture. Every Japanese person lives daily in a rigid framework of obligations and duties to others in the society. The group is always considered more important than the individual, and there is much pressure to conform. I learned that Japanese culture developed gradually over thousands of years based on rice farming. There are two great values people learn if their survival depends on this kind of agriculture. The first is the value of the community. If everyone does not work together at key times in the planting and harvesting cycle, the result is famine. Group effort and harmonious human relations, therefore, are paramount. The second value is process. In rice farming you cannot skip steps and still succeed, nor can you procrastinate and then work extra hard at the end to catch up. Every step of the process must be done efficiently and at the right time, or the harvest and the whole community is in danger.

In recent decades, the social cohesion of Japan has undergone deep erosion. However, to foreigners, Japanese culture is still something very different. Everything in Japan seems to have a process called *kata*, or way of doing things. When something is impossible or simply cannot be changed, the Japanese say "*Shikata ga nai*" which literally means there is no *kata* for doing it. One of the hardest concepts for me to learn was that in Japan, sometimes the process is more important than the results. On the other hand, I began to realize why the Japanese were the world leaders in high quality mass manufacturing, which is all about constantly refining a complex process. Regarding harmonious human relations, I learned that in Japan, to a large extent, your standing in society determines your value as a person. "Face," or how much respect you give and receive, is a gauge of society's evaluation of each individual. For most Japanese, to be shamed or excluded from the group is devastating. In traditional Japanese theater and literature there is a recurring theme of the conflict between personal feelings and social obligations, between romantic love and group loyalty. Suicide is still considered an "honorable" solution when human conflicts between an individual and the group arise that are impossible to resolve in any other way.

At work I found out that in corporate Japan, the group to which you belong to a large extent determines your identity and expected behavior. It is called a "reference" group and must be clearly defined and its borders protected. However, the borders of the reference group could also shift depending on the situation. Understanding and navigating this complex network of obligations took time and energy. Even among close co-workers there were company matters only discussed in the office itself while personal issues related to business were strictly reserved for after-hours meals in restaurants. There was no "rule book" for learning these matters; the understanding was woven into the cultural fabric and foreigners were not expected to understand. Cultural borders applied to matters of faith as well. Although in Japan, Jesus is ranked as one of the most respected spiritual leaders of all time, very few Japanese want to become identified as Christians. Japanese are proud of their highly developed culture. Christianity as a religion is considered non-Japanese, and the decision to follow Jesus outside the borders of Japanese good judgment.

In 1982, when I began working for NEC, I also met Reverend Bob Houlihan, an American with many years of experience in Japan. Among his other responsibilities, Bob was leading a small international fellowship of believers that met in downtown Tokyo. We became friends immediately, and he invited me to join him as his associate in leading the group. Over the years I learned a great deal from Bob and his wife Carolyn. At first, the little fellowship consisted of around a dozen people, mostly foreigners, but as we began to worship

God and pray for the Holy Spirit to visit us each week, the group began to grow. Increasingly, Japanese people were drawn to the freedom they experienced in the presence of God's Spirit.

One of my responsibilities as a pastor was bringing a new form of worship into the song service of our weekly gatherings. I had learned the dynamics of worshipping in song and had internalized a vision of biblical worship from my previous studies. According to the Bible, King David erected a tent in Jerusalem to house the Ark of the Covenant that had been received back from its captivity with the Philistines. He would go into that tent to seek the presence of God and to worship at all hours of the day or night. David instructed Asaph and other psalmists in singing praises to God. Their musical instruments were dedicated to producing songs of worship and of course, David, himself, sang many of his own songs to the Lord. He wrote, "One thing I have asked from the Lord, that I shall seek: That I may dwell in the house of the Lord all the days of my life, to behold the beauty of the Lord and to meditate in His temple" (Psalm 27:4). Our worship in Tokyo was a step towards the restoration of the Spirit of worship that King David so prized. Over the next five years, the fellowship grew to around three hundred people from many backgrounds and from all over Tokyo.

As our numbers grew, I was increasingly faced with new challenges. Bob's responsibilities were regional, and he traveled frequently. Furthermore, after we had worked together for a while, he and Carolyn went to the United States for an extended stay, and I led the growing fellowship as pastor supported by several other businessmen who served as congregational elders. I had to adjust my work schedule to deal with the increased demands on my time, but the main difficulty was with foreign missionaries, ministers, and church leaders I met. Many of them were interested in us because of the growth we were experiencing, and I was always glad to speak to them about what God was doing and how we were handling it. However, if I also began to tell them about my work at NEC, soon I could almost predict the next thing they would say. It was usually something like, "Oh, so you are not in *full-time* ministry?" Then I would try to explain how it was all about time management, and somehow it was working out; I never felt that I managed to convince them. The more I explained, the faster their respect for me as a spiritual leader would decline. Finally, I decided to solve this "problem." I just stopped telling other ministers about my job in Japanese industry.

Inwardly, I knew there was something wrong with this attitude. I was developing a split identity, but at the time, the culture gap between the worlds of business and ministry was too great for many people to cross. They saw the kingdom of God as religion which was "sacred" while the marketplace was "secular" and tainted. No amount of arguing could convince them otherwise. Rita had accepted a job as lecturer in a prestigious university just outside of Tokyo and when she told

154

her students that her husband was a manager in the marketing division of NEC, eighty or ninety students would show up for an evening of discussion. They were eager to know us and learn what brought us to Japan! We learned that in those years, NEC was rated number one among all Japanese companies as a choice for employment among graduating university students. We had many exciting evenings speaking to those bright young students about the kingdom of God.

Throughout our years in Tokyo I continued to struggle with the cultural gap between the world of business and the world of ministry. Eventually, I began to realize that the problem was not just the "worldliness" of business but rather a ministry culture that put almost all its emphasis on only one day of the week. Our goal as ministers was to convince as many people as possible to attend our services on Sunday. That was the "Lord's day" and what we did in our worship service was considered "sacred." What those same people did on Monday was less important because that was considered "secular." Never mind that God's command regarding the Sabbath was to observe a day of total rest. We justified working harder on Sunday than on any other day because we were serving God as His priests! It only occurred to me later that the whole point of having a day of rest is not so that we can exalt that day or its activities, but rather the emphasis of the Sabbath is on God's plan for the rest of the week. Sabbath rest is meant to ensure we have enough wisdom and strength to carry out our King's commands starting on Monday when we go out to meet the challenges of the surrounding culture! Jesus, Himself said, "The Sabbath was made for man, and not man for the Sabbath" (Mark 2:27). R. Paul Stevens, who teaches applied theology at Regent College, wrote an enlightening book entitled, *The Other Six Days*. In it he says, "What makes an activity Christian is not the husk but the heart. Preaching, caring for the flock and equipping the saints can be profoundly secular. Listening to a child, designing a software package, and examining a balance sheet can be profoundly Christian. What makes a work Christian is faith, hope, and love."

While dealing with the cultural divide between business and ministry was difficult, even more challenging was the culture of Japan. The Japanese had rejected Catholicism in the late sixteenth century when it was virtually eradicated by persecution under the warlord Toyotomi Hideyoshi and later by the Tokugawa shoguns. The country was closed to foreigners for 250 years until it was forced open by American gunboats in 1853. In the years that followed, Protestant missionaries began preaching throughout Japan. Today, after 150 years of exposure to Protestant Christianity, still less than one half of one percent of the population is identified as evangelical. The Christian religion is thought to make its adherents "non-Japanese." It is not just that Jesus is seen as a foreigner to the Japanese people. A significant problem is Japanese cultural resistance to Christianity in the religious forms that have been

156

imported from the West.

Japanese people have been told that in order to be "saved," they must leave family, friends, and colleagues at work in order to follow Jesus, their personal Savior. We often sing, "I have decided to follow Jesus. Though none go with me, still I will follow!" This is an important aspect of the gospel; however, many Japanese feel this emphasis on the individual is Western, individualistic, and selfish. I learned later, that some Japanese Christians have an intense interest in Israel and Messianic Jews. They see in the Old Testament that God made a divine covenant with Israel and called the nation to follow Him as an entire people group. As described in the Book of Exodus, the decision to make God King and follow His laws was first and foremost a corporate decision that then impacted every household and individual. Some Japanese say that if God would call Japan in that manner, it would be more "Japanese" to respond as an entire community.

CHAPTER 12

CHAPTER 12

One of my friends during those years in Tokyo was the rabbi of the Jewish Community Center whom we met when we attended services at the synagogue. On several occasions we ate with him and his wife in local restaurants, and I remember the difficulty in finding a place that could prepare food compatible with his dietary restrictions. Among other things, Jewish tradition forbids the eating of pork, shellfish or shrimp, and the mixing of meat and dairy products in the same meal. He would scan the menus looking for types of fish that were "kosher," which means considered fit to eat, and then instruct the chef to cook it on tin foil instead of on a grill that might have been used for non-kosher food.

I went to my Bible and sure enough, among other things God forbade the eating of pigs, birds of prey, and shellfish. This made me curious about the spirit of the biblical dietary laws. I went back to the Sermon on the Mount and tried to understand what Jesus would have taught concerning these laws. In His teaching on God's laws Jesus repeatedly used the phrase, "you have heard...but I say." He would quote one of the commandments Moses had received on Sinai and then give His own ruling as Messiah and King. In each case, Jesus elevated the commandments from the law given to Israel to a higher, perfect level. What would He have said about eating pork?

First of all, 3,000 years ago when God's laws were given, there was no refrigeration and no knowledge of bacteria or microscopic parasites. We know that pigs in the wild will eat just about anything including human feces. I previously thought that indigenous people in places like Borneo were immune to diseases from eating wild boars as well as pigs penned under the houses, but later learned from local doctors that it is not the case. Whole villages have been known to become ill from eating contaminated swine. Certainly in the days of Moses, eating an undercooked pork chop could have resulted in serious illness and even death. The other fish, birds, and animals forbidden to be eaten by God's law are the kind of creatures that feed off the bottom of bodies of water or eat the flesh of dead animals. Again, this kind of wildlife is much more likely to cause health problems than animals like sheep, goats, chickens, cows and fish with fins and scales, which are all allowed. God is very concerned about our physical well-being. Divine health is better than divine healing! I think Jesus would have strictly commanded us to only eat healthy food in every meal out of obedience to God's Spirit. That would mean today that the kind of unhealthy overindulgence in sugars, fats, and salty snacks that characterizes the diet of many in the United

States and other developed countries is a sin!

Food seems to play a prominent role in religions around the world. Why didn't Jesus address it directly in His most important sermon on the Law? I think it's because while food is important, it is not that important in God's kingdom compared with other weightier moral issues. Dietary habits rank high among the surface elements of culture, and not among its root issues. It is a tragedy that millions of children around the world do not have access to uncontaminated water or even adequate nourishment, but I have never heard of a famine that was caused by what is allowed or not allowed to eat by religion. Starvation around the world is almost entirely due to the lack of human justice and compassion, corrupt governments, war, or natural disasters. Less than five percent of the 613 commandments in the laws of Moses are about food. Jesus scolded religious people for not understanding which of God's commandments are more important. He said, "Woe to you, scribes and Pharisees, hypocrites! For you tithe mint and dill and cumin, and have neglected the weightier provisions of the Law: justice and mercy and faithfulness; but these are the things you should have done without neglecting the others" (Matthew 23:23). The apostle Paul followed that up with this saying, "for the kingdom of God is not eating and drinking, but righteousness and peace and joy in the Holy Spirit" (Romans 14:17).

God's command to obey the Sabbath is considered by

many students of the Bible to be among His most important commandments. Orthodox Jews have created a very complex system out of Sabbath observance in their communities in Israel and elsewhere around the world. On one occasion, Rita accompanied an orthodox Jewish woman back to her hotel in Tokyo on a Friday afternoon. She was staying in the forty -story tower of the New Otani Hotel and when they stepped into the elevator the woman looked at her watch and noticed that the Sabbath had just begun. She refused to press the button for her floor because it could cause a tiny spark and break the commandment against lighting a fire on the Sabbath. Because Rita is Jewish, the woman would not allow her to press the button either. As a result, they rode up and down until someone else happened to be staying on the same floor and pushed the right button.

The Sabbath is about resting from work, but what is the Spirit of this law? How did Messianic Jews understand the command to rest on the Sabbath in light of the teaching of Jesus? The New Testament Book of Hebrews was written by a Messianic Jew to other Jewish followers of Jesus of his day. The third and fourth chapters are dedicated to an inspired interpretation of the Sabbath from a New Testament point of view. The writer makes the point that God's rest is entered by faith in God and by ceasing from our own self-initiated and self-directed work. As far as when the Sabbath should be observed, five times in these thirty-five short verses the writer uses the word "today." His point is that Jesus might have taught, "You have heard that the seventh day is holy as a Sabbath to the Lord, but I say unto you, today and everyday should be holy to God and you should cease from vanity and ambitious striving to enter His rest *daily* by fully trusting Him."

After my contract with NEC ended, I was offered a job as the National Marketing Manager for Wang Laboratories in Japan. Wang, an American computer manufacturer listed in the Fortune 500, was opening its own subsidiary in Japan. Suddenly, I was responsible for marketing American-made computers with a Chinese name in the Japanese business market! Here is where I learned firsthand that cultural differences, if not addressed and managed properly, can become business problems. The founder of Wang Labs, Dr. An Wang was an engineering genius and an immigrant to America from China. He blamed Japanese attacks in Shanghai for the deaths of his parents and sister during the second World War and recounted stories of Japanese wartime atrocities in his 1986 biography *Lessons*. When Corporate Marketing wanted Dr. Wang's book translated into local languages and given to top customers in every country, we faced a dilemma regarding how to portray this part of our company founder's life. On another occasion, we wanted to provide an incentive program to our Japanese sales force that was being implemented in Wang offices worldwide. We offered the three top sales achievers huge bonuses. The top performers along with the entire sales department begged us to reconsider. They warned that if implemented, our already low sales performance would actually decline. The successful sales people would be embarrassed, and the poor performers would be shamed. Instead, they argued, give the same incentive to every member of the team irrespective of individual performance. We listened and did what they asked. Sales performance started to improve.

It was a hard battle to find success in the Japanese computer and communications market with a foreign product and limited Japanese language software. Someone at the time said it was like selling "snow to the Eskimos!" At the same time, the congregation where I was pastor was growing in numbers each week, so we organized our elders' and leaders' meetings around breakfast at a hotel near my office. I would meet people for counseling during my lunch hour and teach Bible studies after work. It was a time of increased pressures as well as spiritual growth for me. Through the ongoing struggle to follow God's will, I was learning how obedience to the Spirit of God's laws was an integral part of my business life.

Eventually, I found a market niche for our computer products by locating a portfolio management package produced in New York City. The software designer had once been an award winning musician and arranger for the popular Tonight Show orchestra. He had grown tired of the music industry and sought a new career in high tech. This talented man told me of the close relationship between the laws governing both music arranging and software design! With his product, we began successfully marketing a "turn-key" hardware and software solution to the burgeoning Japanese financial services industry. This professional breakthrough came as a personal encouragement and vindication that God had called me both to ministry and to the marketplace. I was given my company's annual achievement award and began to see the fulfillment of what has been called the "businessman's psalm":

> *How blessed is the man who does not walk in the counsel of the wicked, nor stand in the path of sinners, nor sit in the seat of scoffers! But his delight is in the law of the LORD, and in His law he meditates day and night. He will be like a tree firmly planted by streams of water, which yields its fruit in its season and its leaf does not wither; and in whatever he does, he prospers.*
> (Psalm 1:1-3)

During these years our first child was born. What joy her birth brought to us! We named her Nina, not a Japanese name but unique and easy to pronounce in Japanese. Because her mother is a Jew, according to Jewish traditional law, Nina is Jewish, but with my "dominant" genes she looks Asian. After her birth, the nurses brought her out on a cart with several other babies born that same day. The Japanese babies all looked identical and needed name tags on their feet to identify them!

Even though her Asian features made her look much like the other babies, she was definitely "different," and we knew she would grow up in a much more complex mixture of cultural influences.

CHAPTER 13

CHAPTER 13

My spiritual journey had begun as a search for truth of the kind that is absolute and unchanging. I knew as a young man that without an immovable and eternal reference point, human life is doomed to futility. Without truth, there can ultimately be no lasting love or justice, only survival of the fittest and strongest. My friend John had refused to live in a world like that and ended his life. My own life was changed and salvaged by the revelation that Jesus is my Messiah and personal redeemer. As I continued on with God, I began to realize that He was intent on restoring the true identity in me that had been shattered and lost in my earlier years. The Bible showed me it was revealed to people like the prophet Jeremiah and King David that they were chosen, called, and equipped by God for the challenges in their own lives – before they were born. I began to realize that after being able to correctly identify God, the most important next step spiritually was allowing Him to correctly identify me!

This is particularly clear in the New Testament story, found in Matthew chapter sixteen, when Jesus asked His disciples, "Who do you say that I am?" One of the disciples named Simon immediately answered, "You are the Messiah, the Son of the Living God." Jesus said his answer was correct because of revelation from God, but He followed that up by telling Simon, he would be called Peter, which means a kind of rock, and that he would become a man of strength, stability, and great authority. Apparently, it took some time, because Simon, now called Peter, continued to act in sometimes erratic and irresponsible ways until later, as recorded in the Book of Acts, he emerged as a rock-like leader and one of the foremost spokesmen of the new believing community. I realized that Jesus wasn't assigning something new to Simon, but He was *restoring* the plan that God had at the time of that man's creation. Peter's identity, his spiritual gifts, and his destiny had already been decided, but he still had to choose to follow and accept what God had chosen. It excited me to consider that because of His love, God was determined to develop the plan He had already chosen and designed into me as my Creator.

I also learned that God cares about more than just individuals. We are, after all, social beings, connected to one another in societies and culture is an important part of the "glue" God uses to form those bonds. If humans are to be fully restored to God's original plan, cultures must also be transformed. I saw in Jesus, the Son of God, a perfect man and the embodiment of all that God was seeking through His Law.

172

Jesus became my absolute reference point and the standard by which I could measure myself and all other people. Not that I came out very well in the comparison, but at least now my life had a goal that wouldn't change like the seasons! I began to realize that cultures too need a God-given reference point to save them from the same futility and violence I had experienced on a personal level. At this point, God's choice of Israel as His nation and the prototype of His kingdom on earth began to make a lot of sense. I saw His choice as purposeful rather than one motivated by favoritism.

My grandparents were immigrants to the United States from Japan over one hundred years ago. They settled in southern California but were not allowed to have American citizenship until decades later. My parents were born as the children of these immigrants and grew up as U.S. citizens. Following the Japanese attack on Pearl Harbor, over 110,000 men, women, and children of Japanese descent, most of whom were American-born citizens like many of my relatives, were relocated from the West Coast to internment camps hundreds of miles away in the desert for the duration of the war. They lost property, careers, and most importantly, their freedom. This was a shameful chapter in American history which was described in the Civil Liberties Act of 1988 as being based on "prejudice, war hysteria, and a failure of political leadership."

As a Japanese-American, I grew up as part of a racial minority group in the United States. Later, as a teenager in

Japan, even though I looked completely Japanese, I was a *gaijin*, or cultural foreigner. Now as an Israeli citizen, I definitely fall into a special group. As a result of my life experience, I have become sensitive to racial and cultural prejudice. I understand the values of multiculturalism. However, in order for the dream of cultures mingling together and enriching each other peacefully to be a reality, there must be a higher, heavenly authority defining justice and mercy and providing a fair and objective cultural standard for all. Without this, multiculturalism becomes cultural relativism and anything goes. Who is to say whose cultural values have priority when conflict inevitably arises? Some Americans say ending the life of an unborn fetus is the mother's right. Others say it is murder. Some French citizens want women to be fully veiled in public. Others say that it is not "French" and a security risk. In Saudi Arabia, adultery can result in beheading. In some Western countries the same kind of adultery can make you a celebrity. With no shared cultural standard, we are back to futility, oppression, and survival of the strongest.

Landa Cope, a respected Bible teacher, is the Founder and Executive Director of The Template Institute. TTI seeks to enhance the effectiveness of believers in all areas of society to meet the needs of their communities through their professions. In her newest book, *God, the Bible and Political Justice*, she wrote:

It is impossible to define "justice or mercy" without the Old Testament definition of "justice and mercy." It is impossible to define "political justice" without God's definition in the Old Testament. These concepts do not mean whatever we want them to mean because of our gifts or personality, culture or times. They mean something quite specific to God and only He has the right to define them for us. If we seek to be God's ambassadors then we must represent His policies not the current policies of the world or even in some cases the thinking of Christians in our age.

God's laws and His amazing grace are twin pillars that uphold the entire structure of His unshakable kingdom. They contain the most important values of God's kingdom culture. This powerful and living culture is a spiritual environment designed to mold us into the image of God and to direct our steps along the specific path He has chosen for us. In 1987, we had been living and working in Japan for more than five years. I began to feel strongly the time had come to make a move to fulfill the dream about Israel we had cherished for years. I went to the Israeli embassy and asked for a list of high tech companies marketing their products internationally, and I began to send out letters with my resume. After a while, I started receiving answers in the form of letters written in Hebrew that I couldn't read. My rabbi friend helped me decipher the rejection letters, but finally one company in Haifa wrote back that they were interested in meeting me. It took some time, but eventually Rita and I stopped in Israel while on a business trip to London, and I interviewed with the company. It was called Fibronics, and they made fiber-optic data communication equipment. They immediately made me a job offer. By that time I also had an offer from a large electronics firm near Tel Aviv, but as Rita and I prayed together, we felt God was calling us to Haifa. It seemed to us this was God's chosen place for us to serve and for the unfolding of the next chapter in our lives.

The attraction of Israel for us also had a number of other dimensions. First of all, for Rita, it was the opportunity to find her destiny in the land that God had promised to her people in the words of Scripture. She read the biblical prophecies and promises that God would restore the Jewish people after their long exile and knew it applied to her personally. For me, it was the fulfillment of a spiritual call I had heard years before and I could feel the excitement of participating in one of the greatest historical events of all time. We knew that God had stepped onto the world stage with authority and power uniquely in our generation bringing Jewish people back to their land to demonstrate His covenant faithfulness for the whole world to see.

We also knew that the state of Israel was not going to be a utopian fulfillment of heaven on earth! The great prophet Ezekiel when foretelling the restoration of the Jewish people to the land of Israel said this:

For I will take you from the nations, gather you from all the lands and bring you into your own land. Then I will sprinkle clean water on you, and you will be clean; I will cleanse you from all your filthiness and from all your idols. Moreover, I will give you a new heart and put a new spirit within you; and I will remove the heart of stone from your flesh and give you a heart of flesh. I will put My Spirit within you and cause you to walk in My statutes, and you will be careful to observe My ordinances. You will live in the land that I gave to your forefathers; so you will be My people, and I will be your God. (Ezekiel 36:24-28)

It seems clear from what Ezekiel wrote that God is not expecting the Jewish people to come back to the land morally clean, free of idols, soft of heart, and filled with God's Spirit. This is truly the case with modern Israel. The inspired words of the apostle Paul in the New Testament are also still true today. He wrote:

But it is not as though the word of God has failed. For they are not all Israel who are descended from Israel; nor are they all children because they are Abraham's descendants, but: "Through Isaac your descendants will be named." That is, it is not the children of the flesh who are children of God, but the children of the promise are regarded as descendants. (Romans 9:6-8)

By this, Paul is not writing that believing Gentiles have taken the place of unbelieving Jews in God's plan. Rather, he is saying that within national Israel there is a remnant of believing Jews (today we call them Messianic Jews) who identify both with the Jewish nation and with the kingdom of God. The existence of a believing and praying remnant is vital for the restoration of any nation. According to the Bible, in spite of the gross sins of Sodom, God was willing to spare the entire city for the sake of ten faithful believers! (Genesis 18:26-32) I learned that modern Messianic Jews in Israel were beginning to "stand in the gap" as intercessors for the nation and that their witness is essential for God's plan for Israel to be accomplished. The apostle Paul wrote in His letter to the Romans:

For I do not want you, brethren, to be uninformed of this mystery--so that you will not be wise in your own estimation--that a partial hardening has happened to Israel until the fullness of the Gentiles has come in; and so all Israel will be saved... (Romans 11:25-26a)

In December of 1987 we said goodbye to the fellowship in Tokyo where I had served as pastor for five years. It had grown into a vibrant community of many nationalities. They prayed for us and released us with tears as we set off to a land hardly realizing what would lie in store for us. We went as new immigrants, making *aliyah*, which means ascending to Zion, to a small, embattled country in the Middle East, at the time not yet 40-years-old as a modern nation. We left for Israel as a Jew and a Gentile, not divided by the commandments that demanded separation for the Jews but united by God's Law of the Spirit. Rita and I had grown into the "one new man" described in Ephesians chapter two as a "holy temple in the Lord" and a "dwelling of God in the Spirit." It had been a long journey from the hills of northern New Mexico where we had made our decisions to follow God's leading almost fifteen years earlier. While far from mature, we had learned much about God and His kingdom, and whether we realized it or not, a foundation of faith had been laid in our lives that would help us meet the challenges that awaited us in our new home in northern Israel, on Mt. Carmel, the mountain known for the prophet Elijah's confrontation with the false prophets of his day.

CHAPTER 14

CHAPTER 14

The last question the disciples asked Jesus while He was on earth was, "Lord, is it at this time You are restoring the kingdom to Israel?" (Acts 1:6) Biblical restoration means returning to God's original plan and purpose. Transformation is the word we use to describe the *process* of God's redeeming work. Restoration is God's *goal*. Later, in Jerusalem, the apostle Peter spoke about end time restoration to a group of Jewish worshippers in the courtyard of the Great Temple. He said:

> *Therefore repent and return, so that your sins may be wiped away, in order that times of refreshing may come from the presence of the Lord; and that He may send Jesus, the Christ appointed for you, whom heaven must receive until the period of restoration of all things about which God spoke by the mouth of His holy prophets from ancient time.* (Acts 3:19-21)

Israel was the nation chosen to be God's example of His

kingdom to the world. The history of the Jewish people is the story of their struggle in the grip of this divine selection. The prophet Jeremiah spoke out concerning God's judgment on Israel, but he also prophesied God's ultimate restoration of Israel:

> *"I will restore the fortunes of Judah and the fortunes of Israel and will rebuild them as they were at first. ...For I will restore the fortunes of the land as they were at first,"* says the LORD. (Jeremiah 33:7 and 11)

Paul's writing in the New Testament reveals that God will never change His mind about restoring the original plan for His people Israel, even if they fight against Him.

> *From the standpoint of the gospel they are enemies for your sake, but from the standpoint of God's choice they are beloved for the sake of the fathers; for the gifts and the calling of God are irrevocable.* (Romans 11: 28-29)

I realized that because of God's choice, Israel became His example and the key to God's plan for restoring all the nations of the world to His original plan and purpose. At the same time, I discovered that a growing number of leaders from a variety of different backgrounds are teaching about God's plan of cultural restoration. YWAM's founder, Loren Cunningham, tells the story of how he received his understanding of God's purpose to transform every area of society. He wrote:

In a small cabin on the western slopes of Colorado in August of 1975, our family of four was taking a holiday week. On the second day I received in prayer from the Lord seven "spheres of society" to be used strategically to disciple nations (Matthew 28:18-20). I wrote them on a yellow legal pad: Family (home); Church (religion); Education, Media (electronic and printed); Celebration (arts, entertainment and sports); Economy (research and development, production, sales and service, i.e. commerce) and Government (all branches).

More recently, Cunningham's seven "spheres of society" have been called seven "mountains," "molders of culture," "gates of society," or "areas of influence" by other ministers and writers. While I agree with the strategic direction articulated by these men and women, I feel strongly that in any discussion of God's kingdom and social/cultural restoration through the gospel of the kingdom, Israel and the laws of Israel must have a foundational position. God chose Israel purposefully as His example nation, but the Law was given as a means to humble God's chosen people so that His mercy could be poured out upon all who believe and seek to obey Him. (Romans 11:30-32) Without grappling, as the Jewish apostle Paul did, with the

185

laws God gave to Israel and sharing his inspired conclusions (see Romans chapters seven and eight), there is a danger of prideful "triumphalism" in believers today and everything we say about cultural transformation will lack an authoritative, biblical anchor.

Today we stand at the convergence of two great end time movements: The restoration of God's purposes in the marketplace and the restoration of Israel. The current existence of the nation of Israel and the modern re-emergence of Messianic Jews underscore the fact that God has acted uniquely in our own generation and that the fulfillment of His prophetic words is intended to impact cultures. The Bible is clear about God's final intention to redeem all of Israel (Romans 11:25-27). The danger of ignoring modern Israel and Messianic Jews is that believers will follow an increasingly spiritualized vision of God's kingdom that may create a *subculture* but lacks the credibility and authority to transform non-believing society. The prefix "sub" means *beneath or less than* as when we use the terms *submarine* or *subhuman*. The great challenge for the followers of Jesus today is to view the kingdom of God less as religion and more as a total human culture.

It is also important not to give people an unrealistically optimistic vision of the future. The world will certainly not get better and better everywhere until the return of the Lord. Jesus warned of "wars and rumors of wars" in the end times, saying "these things *must* take place" (Matthew 24:6, emphasis mine).

It is likely that in different locations the world will get much better and much worse simultaneously as we draw nearer to the end of the age. Since the Chinese Red Army's "Long March" in 1934 until now, China has seen both the worst days of its history and in terms of Christian awakening, some of its best in the same generation. In the end times, some nations will prosper, and others will fail. This kind of mixed picture will be played out among many different people groups before the return of the Lord. Jesus once taught a parable about the fruit-bearing grain growing alongside harmful weeds until the final day of harvest. Just before Jesus' return, the Antichrist will have his days of authority and power simultaneous to the rise of the bride-like, end time Church.

Richard Niebuhr's classic book *Christ and Culture* was first published more than half a century ago in 1951, but it still has value for us today. In it he defines the "enduring problem" as the difficult relationship between Christian faith (Christ) and human civilization (culture). Niebuhr offers five different views or approaches to solving the problem: Christ against culture, the Christ of culture, Christ above culture, Christ and culture in paradox, and Christ the transformer of culture. While Niebuhr's writing is a bit dated now and may seem to speak to a different generation, his five views are still helpful because different nations are at different stages in the ongoing tension between biblical faith and human culture. In my book, *God's Tsunami* (first published in 2003), I made an attempt to show how the gospel of God's kingdom, which was launched in Israel 2,000 years ago, has made its way around the world going west from Jerusalem, transforming societies and cultures in the process. Today, this "tsunami" of spiritual and cultural transformation is deeply impacting Africa and Latin America, and especially East Asia. It is destined to sweep its way through Central Asia and the Middle East as it travels westward back to Jerusalem where it began.

This book began with a desire to look back and understand the beginnings of my personal faith in God and my entry point into the culture of His kingdom. Now at the end of the book I am trying to look forward toward what will come in the future. There are a myriad of end time scenarios and speculations about the timing of the Lord's return in circulation today. However, in spite of the many conflicting theories and theologies, there are two things concerning the future about which I feel very certain. The first is that when Jesus returns, He will come as King to rule a kingdom. The second is that He will be returning as a Bridegroom to claim His bride, the body of all true believers. All of us should look forward to the day when God's kingdom is extended over all the kingdoms of the world. We should also all long for and prepare to be among those invited to celebrate at the wedding supper of the Lamb.

With these two focal points in mind, we should all be praying and working toward the restoration of God's kingdom in whatever land or culture to which we are called. Not that

188

we will get everything in perfect order before Jesus returns. Nothing will ever be perfect until He Himself reigns on earth! However, we, His servants, should be about our Father's business in the meantime. Positive changes in any nation's culture can powerfully impact an entire generation of young people and leave an enduring spiritual legacy. Establishing the culture of God's kingdom in our nations is a "blueprint" for our work as believers, while the Spirit of the kingdom's laws written in our hearts defines our character and behavior as a holy bride without spot or blemish. Keeping ourselves aligned with these two goals of the kingdom and the bride will be essential for navigation through the difficult and turbulent times we will all face in the years ahead.

Finally, I have come to see a difference between "revival" and "awakening." Revival is needed when something that once was alive has died and now needs to come alive again. Cultures that once were transformed by God's kingdom and had a biblical heritage but now have lost or are losing that vitality and faith need to be revived. For example, we should pray and work for revival in Europe and America. Nations that have never been widely influenced by the culture of God's kingdom and have never had a biblical foundation for their society need awakening. Japan, China, India, Brazil, and Nigeria are among the examples of these nations. Revival and awakening require very different spiritual strategies and methods. An example could be that when building a house, you need different expertise and equipment when laying the foundation than when you are remodeling and renovating the interior. However, whether through revival or awakening, all people and all cultures everywhere need restoration, that is, a revelation of and return to God's original plan when He created us and placed us in families called nations.

Jesus' disciples' last question resonates now in our hearts as well. They asked, "Lord, is it at this time You are restoring the kingdom to Israel?" Shouldn't we today be asking the Lord that same question about our own nations? It is not ultimately a question concerning only religion, but it is about the spiritual and cultural legacy our generation will leave for the next as that final day approaches when God's angel will sound the trumpet and voices in heaven will say, "The kingdom of the world has become the kingdom of our Lord and of His Messiah; and He will reign forever and ever!" (Revelation 11:15)

REFERENCES

REFERENCES

Chapter 1

Bob Dylan, *Highway 61 Revisited*, Columbia Records, 1965.
Song on album by the same name.

Blowup movie directed by Michelangelo Antonioni. Metro-Goldwyn-Mayer Studios Inc. 1966

Chapter 5

The list of the 613 Commandments in the *Torah* was first compiled by Rabbi Moses ben-Maimon also known as Rambam in his *Mishneh Torah* written in the twelfth century. One version of the list is found on the Internet at: http://www.jewfaq.org/613.htm

Chapter 6

Josh McDowell, *Evidence that Demands a Verdict: Historical Evidences for the Christian Faith*, (San Bernardino: Here's Life Publishers, Inc., 1972)

Chapter 7

Dietrich Bonhoeffer, *The Cost of Discipleship,* translated from German in 1937, (New York: Touchstone, 1995)

Martin Niemöller, *First They Came...*, Poem from Internet: http://en.wikiquote.org/wiki/Martin_Niemöller

Melvyn Bragg, *12 Books that Changed the World*, (London: Hodder & Stoughton, 2006)

Chapter 9

Corrie Ten Boom with John and Elizabeth Sherrill, *The Hiding Place*, (Grand Rapids: Chosen Books, 1971)

TRON, movie written and directed by Steven Lisberger, Released by Walt Disney Pictures, 1982,

Chapter 10

Samuel P. Huntington, *Culture Matters* (New York: Basic Books, 2000), from the foreword

Samuel P. Huntington, *The Clash of Civilizations?* (New York: Foreign Affairs Publishing, Summer 1993)

Edward T. Hall, *Beyond Culture* (New York: Anchor Books, 1977), p. 2.

Thomas J. Peters, *In Search of Excellence* (New York: Harper & Row, 1982), p. 75.

Greg Smith, *Why I Am Leaving Goldman Sachs* (article in *The New York Times*, March 14, 2012)

Chapter 11

Ezra Vogel, *Japan as Number One: Lessons for America* (Lincoln: iUniverse.com Inc., 1979)

R. Paul Stevens, *The Other Six Days* (Grand Rapids: Wm. B. Eerdmans Publishing Co.), p. 248

Chapter 12

An Wang, *Lessons* (Boston: Addison Wesley, 1986)

Chapter 13

The Civil Liberties Act of 1988 signed by President Ronald Reagan was first fulfilled in 1990 when President George H. W. Bush sent a letter of apology to the oldest of the surviving internees. This continued with President Bill Clinton also sending letters to the remaining survivors. Civil Liberties Act of 1988, (www.pbs.org/childofcamp/history/civilact.html)

Landa L. Cope, *God, the Bible and Political Justice*, from her website: http://templateinstitute.com

Chapter 14

Landa L. Cope, *The Old Testament Template: Rediscovering God's Principles for Discipling All Nations* (Burtigny: The Template Institute Press, 2006), from the Foreword by Loren Cunningham, p. 7

Richard Niebuhr, *Christ and Culture* (New York: Harper & Row, 1956)

Peter Tsukahira, *God's Tsunami* (Alachua: Bridge-Logos Publishers, 2008) www.Gods-Tsunami.com

INDEX

INDEX

Look for these other books by
Peter Tsukahira

GOD'S TSUNAMI
Understanding Israel and End-time Revival
www.godstsunami.com

MY FATHER'S BUSINESS
Guidelines for Ministry in the Marketplace
www.amazon.com